VCA-DC

VMware® Certified Associate-Data Center Virtualization on vSphere

Study Guide

VCA-DCV
VMware® Certified Associate-Data Center Virtualization on vSphere
Study Guide

Robert Schmidt

Dane Charlton

A Wiley Brand

Senior Acquisitions Editor: Kenyon Brown
Development Editor: Candace English
Technical Editors: Eric Biller and Brian Atkinson
Production Editor: Christine O'Connor
Copy Editor: Sharon Wilkey
Editorial Manager: Mary Beth Wakefield
Production Manager: Kathleen Wisor
Associate Publisher: Jim Minatel
Media Supervising Producer: Richard Graves
Book Designers: Judy Fung and Bill Gibson
Proofreader: Rebecca Rider
Indexer: Nancy Guenther
Project Coordinator, Cover: Brent Savage
Cover Designer: Wiley

Robert would like to dedicate this book to his wife and three daughters for putting up with him while he was locked in the basement writing it.

Dane would like to dedicate this book to his loving wife and best friend and to thank her for being there for him.

Acknowledgments

The authors would like to acknowledge all of the people at Sybex whose hard work has made this book possible. We would especially like to thank them for their patience with us as we worked through the process of getting a book completed. Our special thanks go out to our acquisitions editor, Kenyon Brown, for bringing us into the project and to our production editor Christine O'Connor and developmental editor Candace Cunningham for keeping us on track and focused on moving forward. We would also like to thank our copy editor, Sharon Wilkey, and our proofreader, Rebecca Rider, for all of the work they have done on this book.

We would also like to thank our coworker and friend Eric Biller for joining the project as our technical editor. His suggestions have helped to keep the text as accurate as possible and have kept us from making a number of obvious and some not so obvious mistakes.

I, Rob Schmidt, would also like to personally thank my coauthor, Dane Charlton, for agreeing to write this book with me and for being one of the first people who got me interested in VMware and their products. By encouraging me to pursue VMware many years ago, he has had a major impact, for the better, on my career and in my life.

About the Authors

Robert Schmidt holds the following certifications: Microsoft Certified Systems Engineer (MCSE), CompTIA Linux+, Novell Certified Network Administrator (CNA), VMware Certified Administrator (VCA), and VMware Certified Professional (VCP 2.5, 3, 4, 5). In the past, he has held the Certified Information Systems Security Professional (CISSP) and the Cisco Certified Network Administrator (CCNA) certifications.

Robert has over 20 years of experience working with information technology and has spent the last 10 years specializing in virtualization. He has been heavily involved in several large virtualization initiatives and continues to work in the Cleveland, Ohio area. He has been married for 19 years and has three daughters.

Dane Charlton holds the following certifications: VMware Certified Professional (VCP 2.5, 3, 4, 5), Microsoft Certified IT Professional (Enterprise Messaging), and Microsoft Certified Technology Specialist (Exchange). In the past, he has held the Microsoft Certified Systems Engineer (MCSE), Certified Novell Engineer (CNE 2, 3, 4), and Bay Networks Certification.

Dane has over 25 years of experience working with information technology for small and large companies. For the last 15 years, he's been supporting virtualization efforts along with large messaging environments in Akron, Ohio. Dane has been married for 15 years and has three children and eight grandchildren.

Contents at a Glance

Contents

Introduction

Welcome to the *VCA-DCV: VMware Certified Associate-Data Center Virtualization on vSphere Study Guide* for exam VCAD510. The purpose of this book is to help you prepare for the VCA-DCV exam by becoming familiar with the challenges that businesses face and the tools and technologies that are provided by VMware to help meet those challenges. Even though the book is primarily designed to help with the VCA-DCV, we hope it will also help administrators better understand some of the tools they could be using to make their lives easier as well as gain better insight into the tools that they are using.

We (the authors, Dane Charlton and Robert Schmidt) have extensive backgrounds in information technology and specialize in managing and maintaining large virtual environments. Together we have over 45 years of technology experience that we hope to share in this book.

The book contains all of the information you need to pass the VCA-DCV exam. It also includes notes and warnings to help reduce issues you may be experiencing in your own environment. By studying for and passing this exam, you will gain insight that will make you more valuable in your current position and more likely to get recognized and promoted.

In the remainder of this section, we will present some of the facts about the exam, give some commonsense tips for taking the exam, and review the process for registering.

Exam Facts

Here are some facts for the VCA-DCV: VMware Certified Associate-Data Center Virtualization on vSphere Exam, VCAD510:

- The VCA-DCV exam is administered by Pearson VUE but is taken from home over the Internet.
- There are 50 multiple-choice questions.
- The passing score is 300 out of 500.
- There is a time limit of 75 minutes for the exam.
- There is a short survey before the exam begins (taking the survey does not use any of the available 75 minutes).
- If you do not pass the exam, you can retake it as many times as you want; no waiting period is required.

Tips for Taking the VCA-DCV Exam

Here are some general tips for improving the odds on your certification exam:

- Read each question carefully. Although the test is not written to be confusing, at times the obvious choice is not the correct choice.

- Make sure you answer each question. Any unanswered questions are considered wrong, so you are better off making an educated guess than leaving a question unanswered.

- If you are unsure of the correct answer for a question, use a process of elimination to remove any obviously incorrect answers first. Once you have eliminated the obviously incorrect answers, take an educated guess from the remaining answers.

- If you are unsure about a question, select the answer you think is most likely to be correct, mark it for review, and come back to it at a later time.

- Get a good night's sleep the night before the exam. This will help you be more alert and think more clearly during the exam.

- Before scheduling the exam, review the Exam Blueprint to make sure you understand each of the objectives and review any you are unsure of:

  `https://mylearn.vmware.com/mgrReg/plan.cfm?plan=41162&ui=www_cert`

Exam Registration

You must take the following steps to register for the VCA-DCV exam:

1. Using a browser, navigate to the VCA-DCV web page:

   `https://mylearn.vmware.com/mgrReg/plan.cfm?plan=41162&ui=www_cert`

2. Click the Request Exam Authorization option. If you do not have a mylearn account, you will be prompted to create one.

3. Once your authorization for the exam is confirmed, you will be presented with your first name, last name, and candidate ID.

4. Go to the Pearson VUE website (`www.pearsonvue.com`). Select the For Test Takers option and then input **VMware** as your program.

5. Select VCA-DCV and enter your first name, last name, and candidate ID.

6. Once you have registered for the exam, keep an eye out for an email with a link to the exam. You will have three days from registering to follow this link and take the exam.

   VMware requires certification candidates to accept the terms of a nondisclosure agreement before taking certification exams.

Who Should Read This Book?

This book is intended for individuals who want to earn their VCA-DCV: VMware Certified Associate-Data Center Virtualization on vSphere certification. It would also be useful for any VMware administrators who would like to have an introduction to VMware technologies that they may not use on a day-to-day basis in their current positions.

What's Inside?

Here is a glance at what's in each chapter:

Chapter 1: Intro to Virtualization   Introduces some of the basic concepts of VMware virtualization.

Chapter 2: VMware Solutions   Shows the types of challenges that businesses face and some of the VMware tools that can help them meet these challenges.

Chapter 3: vSphere Core Components   Introduces core technologies that the VMware virtualization suite comprises.

Chapter 4: Storage in a VMware Environment   Introduces you to the types of storage that exist in a virtual environment and the tools for managing this storage.

Chapter 5: Networking in a VMware Environment   Covers the types of networking technologies that are used in virtual environments and how to use VMware tools to manage them.

Chapter 6: Business Challenges Meet VMware Solutions   Presents real-world scenarios of issues that businesses face and discusses the VMware technologies and products that can be used to mitigate these challenges.

What's Included with the Book

This book includes many helpful items intended to prepare you for the VCA-DCV: VMware Certified Associate-Data Center Virtualization on vSphere certification.

Assessment Test   The Assessment Test at the conclusion of the book's introduction can be used to quickly evaluate where you are with VMware virtualization products. This test should be taken prior to beginning your work in this book, and it should help you identify areas in which you are either strong or weak. Note that these questions are purposely more simple than the types of questions you may see on the exams.

Objective Map and Opening List of Objectives   At the start of this book is a detailed exam objective map showing you where each of the exam objectives is covered in this book. In addition, each chapter opens with a list of the exam objectives it covers. Use these to see exactly where each of the exam topics is covered.

Exam Essentials   The end of each chapter provides a brief overview of the concepts covered in the chapter. We recommend reading through these sections carefully to check your recollection of each topic and returning to any sections of the chapter you're not confident about having mastered.

Chapter Review Questions   Each chapter includes review questions. The material for these questions is pulled directly from information that was provided in the chapter. These questions are based on the exam objectives, and they are similar in difficulty to items you might receive on the VMware VCA-DCV exam.

Interactive Online Learning Environment and Test Bank

The interactive online learning environment that accompanies *VCA-DCV: VMware Certified Associate—Data Center Virtualization on vSphere Study Guide* for exam VCAD510 provides a test bank with study tools to help you prepare for the certification exam and increase your chances of passing it the first time! The test bank includes the following:

Sample Tests   All of the questions in this book are provided: the **Assessment Test,** which you'll find at the end of this introduction, and the **Chapter Tests** that include the Review Questions at the end of each chapter. In addition, there are two **Practice Exams.** Use these questions to test your knowledge of the Study Guide material. The online test bank runs on multiple devices.

Flashcards   Questions are provided in digital flashcard format (a question followed by a single correct answer). You can use the flashcards to reinforce your learning and provide last-minute test prep before the exam.

Other Study Tools   A glossary of key terms from this book is available as a fully searchable PDF.

Go to http://sybextestbanks.wiley.com to register and gain access to this interactive online learning environment and test bank with study tools.

How to Use This Book

If you want a solid foundation for preparing for VCA-DCV exam VCAD510, then look no further. We've spent a lot of time putting together this book with the sole intention of helping you to pass the exam!

This book is loaded with valuable information. You'll get the most out of your study time if you follow this approach:

1. Take the assessment test immediately following this introduction. (The answers are at the end of the test, but no peeking!) It's OK if you don't know any of the answers—that's what this book is for. Carefully read over the explanations for any question you get wrong, and make note of the chapters where that material is covered.

2. Study each chapter carefully, making sure you fully understand the information and the exam objectives listed at the beginning of each one. Again, pay extra-close attention to any chapter that includes material covered in questions you missed on the assessment test.

3. Answer all the review questions related to each chapter. Specifically, note any questions that confuse you, and study the corresponding sections of the book again. And don't just skim these questions—make sure you understand each answer completely.

4. Test yourself using all the electronic flashcards. This is a brand-new and updated flashcard program to help you prepare for the latest VCA-DCV exam, and it is a really great study tool.

Learning every bit of the material in this book is going to require that you apply yourself with a good measure of discipline, so try to set aside the same time period every day to study, and select a comfortable and quiet place to do so. If you work hard, you will be surprised at how quickly you learn this material. If you follow the steps listed here and study with the review questions, practice exams, and electronic flashcards, you will increase your chances of passing the exam.

How to Contact Sybex

Sybex strives to keep you supplied with the latest tools and information that you need for your work. Please check the website at http://sybextestbanks.wiley.com.

You can contact Robert Schmidt by email at rschmidt1300@yahoo.com.

You can contact Dane Charlton by email at charles.twin@gmail.com.

VCAD510 Exam Objectives

Objective	Chapter
Section 1—Explain Data Center Virtualization Concepts and How They Solve Typical Business Challenges	
Objective 1.1—Identify and Explain the Concept of Data Center Virtualization	1
■ Explain data center virtualization	
■ Differentiate physical and virtual data center components	
■ Identify data center virtualization benefits	
Objective 1.2—Identify Common Business Challenges Addressed By VMware Solutions	2
■ Identify common availability challenges	
■ Identify common management challenges	
■ Identify common scalability challenges	
■ Identify common optimization challenges	

Objective	Chapter
Section 2—Identify, Explain, and Differentiate vSphere Technologies	
Objective 2.1—Identify vSphere Core Components	3
• Explain the concept and capabilities of a virtual machine	
• Identify the purpose of ESXi and vCenter Server	
• Differentiate VMware migration technologies	
• Differentiate VMware availability technologies	
• Explain the concepts of clusters and resource pools	
• Identify and explain common VMware data center products	
Objective 2.2—Differentiate vSphere Storage Technologies	4
• Differentiate physical and virtual storage	
• Explain the use of shared storage in a vSphere implementation	
• Differentiate VMFS and NFS datastores	
• Explain thin provisioning	
• Differentiate VMware disaster-recovery/disaster-tolerance technologies	
• Identify capabilities of Storage I/O Control	
• Identify capabilities of Storage DRS	
• Explain VMware virtual storage technologies	
Objective 2.3—Differentiate vSphere Networking Technologies	5
• Differentiate physical and virtual networking	
• Differentiate VMware virtual switch technologies	
• Identify VMware virtual switch components	
• Identify common virtual switch policies	
• Identify capabilities of Network I/O Control	
Section 3—Correlate VMware Data Center Virtualization Solutions with Specific Business Challenges	
Objective 3.1—Apply VMware Data Center Virtualization Solutions to Common Business Challenges	2, 6
• Apply VMware data center virtualization technologies to resolve common availability challenges	
• Apply VMware data center virtualization technologies to resolve common management challenges	
• Apply VMware data center virtualization technologies to resolve common optimization challenges	
• Apply VMware data center virtualization technologies to resolve common scalability challenges	
• Differentiate SMB and enterprise challenges and solutions	

Assessment Test

1. Which VMware technology can be used to migrate a virtual machine from one ESXi host to a different ESXi host?
   A. Distributed Resource Scheduler (DRS)
   B. Storage vMotion (svMotion)
   C. vMotion
   D. vSphere Replication

2. What challenges are resolved by leveraging vSphere? (Choose two.)
   A. Office politics
   B. Reducing power consumption
   C. Reducing the number of physical devices
   D. Generating revenue

3. You support all of the Windows servers in your company. However, there are only six servers in the entire organization. Two of the six servers run a critical application that must be up at all times. You decide to use VMware software to gain the benefits of virtualization. What VMware solution do you suggest to the application owner to address the uptime requirement?
   A. vCenter high availability (HA)
   B. vSphere Site Recovery Manager (SRM)
   C. vSphere Data Protection
   D. Fault tolerance (FT)

4. Mike is an administrator for a large corporation that has two main corporate offices and several branch offices spread across the country. The corporate offices use a number of VMware technologies that require the use of shared storage on the ESXi hosts. Purchasing new shared storage arrays for all the branch offices would be cost-prohibitive. Which of the following VMware technologies could be used to allow the branch offices to have shared storage without the additional cost of adding new storage arrays?
   A. Memory ballooning
   B. vFlash
   C. vSphere Storage Appliance (VSA)
   D. vSphere Replication

5. Which of the following is not a disadvantage of using local storage in a VMware environment?

    A. vMotion does not work for virtual machines stored on local disks.

    B. Local storage can be relatively expensive when compared to other storage types like Fibre Channel.

    C. High availability (HA) cannot be used for virtual machines stored on local storage.

    D. Local storage cannot be configured as a raw device mapping (RDM).

6. What VMware technology can you use to segment network traffic by creating multiple resource pools on a single network uplink?

    A. Virtual switch

    B. vCenter

    C. Network I/O Control

    D. vMotion

7. Which one of the following is an example of a scalability challenge?

    A. Ability to use features that require shared storage at branch offices

    B. Compliance monitoring of the environment

    C. Hardware failures

    D. Reclaiming unused storage that has been allocated to servers

8. IT management around the world is putting pressure on IT departments to do what? (Choose two.)

    A. Reduce operating cost

    B. Increase the number of physical servers

    C. Improve system availability

    D. Increase the complexity of the data center

9. An application owner is running clustering software that will restart his protected applications on another server if the server they are running on fails. What is a VMware solution that can protect a virtual server from long outages due to hardware failures?

    A. Virtual SAN

    B. High availability (HA)

    C. VMware Distributed Resource Scheduler (DRS)

    D. vSphere Site Recovery Manager

10. Bill is an administrator at Cheap Guy Corp. He has an ESXi host that currently has the maximum amount of memory that it will hold but is still experiencing memory caching to disk. There is no money in the budget for a new server until next year but there is a relatively small amount of money available. Which of the following VMware technologies can help Bill mitigate the memory issues he is having until he can get a new server in the next fiscal year?

   A. Hot add

   B. Thin provisioning

   C. vFlash

   D. vSphere Storage Appliance (VSA)

11. Which of the following disk provision types performs disk zeroing as production writes are occurring? (Choose all that apply.)

   A. Thick provision eager zeroed

   B. Thick provision lazy zeroed

   C. Thin provision

   D. Both B and C

12. Which one of these is not a feature of a distributed virtual switch?

   A. Private VLANs

   B. Hypervisor

   C. Network vMotion

   D. Link aggregation

13. Which one of the following would be considered an example of an availability challenge?

   A. Failed application upgrades

   B. Load balancing server workloads

   C. Locating performance-based bottlenecks

   D. Reducing power usage whenever possible

14. What types of devices can you virtualize? (Choose all that apply.)

   A. Switches

   B. Uninterruptable power supplies

   C. Physical servers

   D. Routers

15. You are brought in to design a virtualization solution for a small company. The company has about 30 physical servers that utilize an average of 10 percent CPU and 20 percent of the memory. After explaining that one of the benefits of virtualization is higher hardware utilization, you are asked what VMware product can monitor virtual machine resources to make sure they are configured most efficiently. What product do you suggest?

    A. High availability (HA)

    B. Virtual SAN

    C. vSphere Data Protection

    D. vCenter Operations Manager (vCOPS)

16. Ken is a system administrator for a large accounting firm with many servers. He is concerned that their standard method of backing up and restoring physical servers may not be the best option for backing up and restoring his virtual machines. Which VMware technology would you recommend that Ken use to back up and restore his virtual servers?

    A. Fault tolerance (FT)

    B. High availability (HA)

    C. vSphere Data Protection

    D. vSphere Replication

17. During which of the following operations can the disk provisioning of a drive be set?

    A. Adding a new drive to an existing virtual machine

    B. When an existing virtual machine is cloned

    C. When using Storage vMotion (svMotion)

    D. All of the above

18. What is the one thing required to connect a virtual machine to a virtual switch?

    A. Storage adapter

    B. Enterprise license

    C. vCenter Server

    D. Port group

19. Which one of the following would be considered an example of an optimization challenge?

    A. Compliance monitoring of the environment

    B. Hardware failures

    C. Locating performance-based bottlenecks

    D. The ability to quickly deploy new servers

20. Which hardware devices need to be directly accessed by virtual machines?

    A. Network cards

    B. Storage infrastructure

    C. Memory

    D. None of the above

21. You are having an argument with a coworker about the advantages and disadvantages of a hosted hypervisor. What is the biggest reason to use a hosted hypervisor?

   A. A hosted hypervisor does not need to run on top of an OS.

   B. A hosted hypervisor allows access to hardware that may not be accessible by a bare-metal hypervisor.

   C. A hosted hypervisor is much smaller.

   D. A hosted hypervisor is faster than a bare-metal hypervisor.

22. The Windows Server Support Team at a medium-sized company needs to upgrade a number of their Windows 2008 R2 virtual servers from 8 GB of memory to 12 GB of memory. Because these are production servers, they cannot be taken down during the day and any outages need to be scheduled in the middle of the night. The team has asked whether these upgrades can be performed without taking the virtual servers down, so they can be upgraded at a more reasonable time. Which of the following VMware technologies would allow the upgrades to be performed without a server outage?

   A. High availability (HA)

   B. Hot add

   C. Snapshots

   D. vSphere Replication

23. Which of the following best describes the vSphere Storage Appliance (VSA)?

   A. A VMware technology that can be used to aggregate unused disks on ESXi hosts and use them as shared storage

   B. A VMware disaster-recovery solution that can restore an entire datacenter with the pressing of a few buttons

   C. A VMware technology that allows storage arrays to be separated into different performance classes depending on the characteristics of the storage array

   D. A VMware technology that load balances virtual machine storage demand across storage arrays to remove the problem of hot spots, whereby one storage array is overused while others go underused

24. You work for a large company that is implementing traffic shaping on the network. You are requested to implement traffic-shaping policies on all outbound virtual machine traffic. What do you need to implement this?

   A. Standard virtual switch

   B. Distributed virtual switch

   C. Multiple port groups defined on a distributed switch

   D. Multiple network uplinks on a switch

25. Which of the following best describes vSphere Replication?

   A. A hardware-independent solution to replicate a virtual machine or group of virtual machines to another site

   B. A VMware backup solution that allows virtual machines to be easily backed up and restored

   C. A VMware solution that allows two virtual machines to act together for zero down-time in the event one of them fails

   D. A VMware solution that allows a virtual machine to restart on a different host if the host it is running on fails

26. What is the role of the hypervisor on a physical host?

   A. To isolate the installed applications from the underlying operating system

   B. To convert physical devices into software representations

   C. To manage deployments of new virtual machines

   D. To isolate the operating system and applications from the underlying hardware

27. One of your coworkers is new to the virtualization game. How do you explain the difference between how networking works with physical servers versus virtual machines?

   A. There is no difference.

   B. Virtual machines can talk only to other virtual machines on the same host.

   C. A specific physical network card is configured for each virtual machine.

   D. Virtual machines are connected through a port group that has a physical network card uplink.

28. The virtualization engineers at ABC Corp. size new virtual machines based on requirements that are given to them by their Windows Server and Linux Server teams. These teams routinely ask for larger drives than they will use, and it is starting to become an issue as LUNs are filling up with unused storage and additional LUNs are not in the budget. Which VMware technology can the virtualization engineers use to reclaim unused storage on the existing virtual machines and keep new virtual machines from taking up more storage than they need?

   A. Snapshots

   B. Thick provisioning

   C. Thin provisioning

   D. vFlash

29. Which of the following disk provision types allows the most virtual machines to fit on a given datastore?

   A. Thick provision eager zeroed

   B. Thick provision lazy zeroed

   C. Thick provision fully zeroed

   D. Thin provision

30. You work for a company that relies heavily on tagging network traffic as VLANs all through the network infrastructure. What VMware object allows policies for tagging like this?

A. Standard virtual switch

B. Distributed virtual switch

C. Virtual machines

D. vCenter Server

31. You are the IT department for a small company that has four ESXi hosts connected in a cluster. You have vCenter Server managing the cluster. You convince upper management that you need a new ESXi host. You install the ESXi hypervisor on the new server and put it in the existing cluster. What is the best way to spread out the virtual machines to take advantage of the new ESXi host?

A. ESXi hypervisor

B. vSphere Distributed Resource Management (DRS)

C. vSphere Data Protection

D. vSphere fault tolerance

32. Which one of the following would be considered a management challenge?

A. Compliance monitoring of the environment

B. Load balancing storage workloads

C. Locating performance-based bottlenecks

D. The need for very high uptime servers

33. In the context of virtualization, the term *conversion* describes what?

A. Consolidation

B. Virtualization of the physical network interface card

C. Hypervisor

D. The migration from physical to virtual

34. BIG Corp. is a large company that has many ESXi hosts and is expanding quickly. In its efforts to quickly build new ESXi hosts, BIG Corp. has experienced issues as the vSwitches on the hosts have been incorrectly configured. The company has also had to make networking changes, which have required reconfiguring the vSwitches on every ESXi host. Which VMware technology would you recommend to make it easier to perform the initial vSwitch configurations on the ESXi hosts and simplify any changes to the vSwitches that are required?

A. Distributed vSwitches (dvSwitches)

B. Distributed Resource Scheduler (DRS)

C. Snapshots

D. vCenter Configuration Manager

35. Which of the following VMware technologies does not move virtual machines from one datastore to another?

    A. Storage vMotion (svMotion).

    B. Storage DRS (sDRS).

    C. High availability (HA).

    D. All of the above move virtual machines from one datastore to another.

36. What has to happen before any distributed virtual switch polices regarding network shares are enforced?

    A. The existence of at least one standard switch.

    B. More than one uplink has to exist.

    C. Network traffic must be moving in both directions.

    D. Contention of network traffic.

Answers to Assessment Test

1. Answer: C. vMotion can be used to move a virtual machine from one ESXi host to another ESXi host with no downtime for the virtual machine. vMotion can be extremely useful when performing hardware maintenance or performing patching on ESXi hosts.

2. Answer: B, C. Reducing power consumption is a big advantage provided by consolidation. Reducing the number of physical devices is the definition of consolidation. vSphere can help your company save revenue but does not generate revenue. There is no guarantee that office politics will be affected in any way. We can dream, though.

3. Answer: D. Fault tolerance (FT) is the VMware solution to this problem. None of the other answers would work for this.

4. Answer: C. The vSphere Storage Appliance (VSA) can be used to aggregate unused disks on ESXi hosts and use them as shared storage. This is very effective for branch offices that do not have shared storage.

5. Answer: B. Local storage is relatively inexpensive when compared to other storage types like Fibre Channel.

6. Answer: C. Network I/O Control isolation is used to segment traffic by creating multiple resource pools.

7. Answer: A. As many organizations scale up, they find they need to use different solutions at their branch offices than they do at their main offices and datacenters due to the high cost of infrastructure. The vSphere Storage Appliance (VSA) allows the use of local ESXi host drives as if they were shared storage. By implementing VSA, companies can use the same solutions in their branch offices as they do in their main offices and datacenters, even if they require shared storage.

8. Answer: A, C. The two most common pressures from IT management are to reduce operating costs and improve system availability. These two pressures used to be mutually exclusive.

9. Answer: B. Many organizations that rely on Microsoft Cluster Service to protect an application would be best served by just relying on high availability (HA).

10. Answer: C. Bill could use the limited funds he has to add a solid-state drive to the ESXi host and then implement vFlash on the host. vFlash allows virtual machines to use solid-state drives on the ESXi host as their cache to increase performance and reduce the impact of memory swapping.

11. Answer: D. Both thick provision lazy zeroed and thin provision drives perform zeroing during production writes. Only thick provision eager zeroed drives are fully zeroed when they are created.

12. Answer: B. The hypervisor is the layer that abstracts physical server hardware from virtual machines. The hypervisor is an operating system like ESXi and is not a part of a distributed virtual switch.

13. Answer: A. A failed application upgrade could result in an application not being available to the users who rely on it. Taking a snapshot of a virtual machine before upgrading the application running on it can help reduce the chances of an application upgrade causing an application outage.

14. Answer: A, C, D. All of these devices can be virtualized except for uninterruptable power supplies (UPS).

15. Answer: D. vCenter Operations Manager (vCOPS) does a good job of letting you zero in on inefficiencies of virtual machines. This really makes sense when many physical servers have four or eight CPU cores and really need only one or two.

16. Answer: C. vSphere Data Protection is a VMware solution for backing up and restoring virtual machines. It is much easier to restore a virtual machine with vSphere Data Protection than with more-traditional file backup methods.

17. Answer: D. Disk provisioning can occur when creating a new virtual machine, when adding a new drive to an existing virtual machine, when cloning an existing virtual machine, or when using Storage vMotion (svMotion) on a virtual machine.

18. Answer: D. A port group is required to connect a virtual machine to a virtual switch. This is true whether the virtual switch is distributed or not.

19. Answer: C. As your computing environment scales up and becomes more complex, it can become more difficult to locate performance-based bottlenecks and get them resolved. vCenter Operations Manager (vCOPS) can help identify these issues in large virtual environments so they can be quickly resolved.

20. Answer: D. Virtual machines do not need direct access to any physical hardware devices. Virtual machines just need to communicate with the hypervisor, which does talk to physical hardware devices and the other virtual machines on the ESXi host.

21. Answer: B. A hosted hypervisor makes sense if you need access to hardware that a bare-metal hypervisor does not. A hosted hypervisor is not necessarily smaller in size. And, even if it is, that is not a good reason to choose a hosted hypervisor.

22. Answer: B. Hot add allows additional CPUs or memory to be added to running virtual machines, allowing them to scale up to higher workloads without downtime. The main condition with hot add is that it must be supported by the operating system of the virtual machine. Most newer operating systems support hot add.

23. Answer: A. The vSphere Storage Appliance (VSA) is a VMware technology that can be used to aggregate unused disks on ESXi hosts and use them as shared storage. This can help to bring shared storage to smaller environments where it would not be cost-effective and to branch offices of larger organizations.

24. Answer: A. The only thing you need is a standard virtual switch for this. A standard virtual switch can be leveraged to implement outbound traffic shaping (not inbound).

25. Answer: A. vSphere Replication is a hardware-independent way to replicate virtual machines to other sites for disaster recovery. It is not meant as a backup solution.

26. Answer: D. The hypervisor separates the physical hardware from the operating system and installed applications. The operating system and installed applications are together. The hypervisor plays the part of resource traffic cop.

27. Answer: D. All virtual machines that need to talk on the network are connected to a port group that has a network uplink. The ESXi host can share the physical network card with many virtual machines.

28. Answer: C. Thin provisioning allows virtual machines to conserve disk space by consuming only the amount of space they need and expanding as more space is needed. New drives can be configured for thin provisioning when they are created, and existing drives can be converted to thin provisioning by using Storage vMotion and specifying Thin Provisioning as the disk type.

29. Answer: D. A thin provision disk consumes only the space on a datastore that is actually being used, while both thick provision eager zeroed and thick provision lazy zeroed take up all the space that is allocated to them as soon as they are created. Thick provision fully zeroed is not a real option for disk provisioning.

30. Answer: B. Policies that are available on the distributed virtual switch include resource allocation, monitoring, traffic filtering, and yes, VLAN tagging (802.1Q).

31. Answer: B. Although you can manually move virtual machines to the new host, DRS provides a better mechanism. DRS can spread the load over multiple ESXi hosts and do it automatically.

32. Answer: A. Many organizations are highly regulated, and making sure their environments meet compliance requirements is a significant management challenge. vCenter Configuration Manager can help monitor the environment for unexpected changes that could cause it to be out of compliance.

33. Answer: D. A physical data center would need to be converted into a virtual representation. The process is a *conversion*. VMware has a migration program that converts physical servers directly into virtual servers. Not surprisingly, the product is call VMware Converter.

34. Answer: A. Distributed vSwitches (dvSwitches) are a form of virtual switch that can be configured once, and then as additional ESXi hosts are added, they can be easily connected to these dvSwitches to simplify virtual switch creation. Since these dvSwitches are created once and then used on multiple ESXi hosts, they can reduce the occurrence of configuration errors when compared to creating standard vSwitches on each ESXi host.

35. Answer: C. High availability (HA) does not move virtual machines from one datastore to another. When HA restarts a virtual machine, it is still located on the same datastore.

36. Answer: D. If there is no contention, there is no need for these policies. This is the same as resource configuration on CPU or memory. If there is no contention, there is no need to enforce rules you have configured (for the most part).

VCA-DCV

VMware® Certified Associate-Data Center Virtualization on vSphere

Study Guide

Chapter

1

Intro to Virtualization

THE VCA-DCV TOPICS COVERED IN THIS CHAPTER INCLUDE THE FOLLOWING:

✓ **Identify and explain the concept of data center virtualization**

- Explain data center virtualization
- Differentiate physical and virtual data center components
- Identify data center virtualization benefits

This chapter covers the basic concepts of data center virtualization and challenges addressed by that virtualization. You'll look at physical data center components and learn to differentiate between them. Then you will go over the advantages of data center virtualization and specific VMware products. (We discuss these specific products further in future chapters.) Finally, you will learn about some of the tools available online to help with the VCAD510 exam. By the end of this chapter, you will be able to define *data center virtualization*, differentiate between physical and virtual components, and list specific benefits of data center virtualization.

What Is Data Center Virtualization?

This section presents data center virtualization in a broad sense. It provides some background in order to give some context and introduces some of the vocabulary so you can join in on virtualization conversations around the water cooler.

The short explanation of *data center virtualization* is that it is a combination of physical hardware converted to software to allow greater utilization of the physical hardware, thereby increasing efficiency and reducing the amount of hardware needed. Data center virtualization is abstract—there is no physical entity that you can touch. Fortunately, virtual data center components can be considered the same as physical data center components. There are more similarities between a physical network card and a virtual network card than there are differences.

Today's modern data center includes virtualization at the root. Many devices that used to be physical can now exist totally in the virtual world. By leveraging virtualization, many logical devices can be created from one physical device. For example, the network card in a VMware ESXi host, through virtualization, can be many network cards—a virtual network card presented to each virtual machine on the host. Similarly, all the physical hardware devices that make up the physical host that is running the VMware hypervisor (ESXi) are presented to each virtual machine on the host.

The Hypervisor

In the VMware world, the *hypervisor* is the ESXi software. A hypervisor like ESXi plays the traffic cop for software resources. This allows multiple virtual machines to share the same physical hardware, which is the definition of consolidation.

Of course, this is only where the good stuff starts.

Virtualization Then and Now

I have been working with computers for a really long time. When I started working with computers, a 10 MB hard drive provided a lot of storage. Most business computers had between 640 KB and 1 MB of memory. A lot has changed over the years, but one thing remains the same: businesses want to get as much return on investment as possible. It is easy to see the benefit of saving space or a little memory when you multiply that amount by a large number of computers. Not to mention the savings on data center power and cooling.

Back then, a company that specced out a new computer would have to buy a server that could handle the load at peak load time (Figure 1.1). That is, a server would have to be able to handle the most work requested of it at any given time. For example, if a new web server was needed, it might have to be able to handle 500 simultaneous users once a day. So, the new server would need to be big enough to handle that load even though that load occurred only once a day. As a result, companies typically had a large number of servers, and most of the servers were idle a lot of the time.

FIGURE 1.1   Before virtualization, servers were sized for peak load.

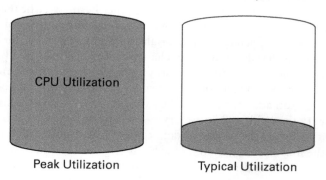

Peak Utilization   Typical Utilization

For this reason, virtualization makes a lot of sense. Virtualization is nothing new. Large mainframe companies such as IBM came up with the idea of virtualization decades ago and initially used it as a development environment more than anything else.

When virtualization started being leveraged in the PC world, it also was primarily used for development. When I started using VMware Workstation, it was an easy way to bring up an entire infrastructure on a PC. This represented a tremendous advantage. Now you can develop a solution that requires domain controllers, file servers, DNS servers, and application servers without buying a lot of hardware. Even when VMware ESX was released, many companies realized this could save them a lot of money but used it only for development environments. In fact, VMware once had an enterprise solution to provide developers with isolated environments. It was called VMware Lab Manager. Lab Manager was discontinued a few years ago. The functionality of Lab Manager was replaced by vCloud Director. However, vCloud Director requires Enterprise Plus licensing and takes some effort to reproduce what Lab Manager did.

Some companies, however, realized the potential of using VMware for real production environments. And the perception of VMware changed. Now, any company with a lot of servers has to at least entertain the idea of using virtualization. And companies that leverage virtualization see some amazing benefits. In fact, now the goal is more than a return on investment; it is the flexibility that virtualization provides along with some enterprise-level solutions from VMware.

I troubleshoot servers all day. When an application owner needs help with a server, I really hope it is a virtual server, because troubleshooting a virtual server can be much easier than troubleshooting a physical server. When troubleshooting a physical server, the problem is often a hardware or driver issue. I don't see, or rarely see, those kinds of problems with virtual servers. And, as the percentage of virtual servers increases in a company, some things just get easier. Now there is very little reason to have any physical application servers.

It was not too long ago that many companies deployed VMware but did not trust it enough to run business-critical applications such as enterprise email systems (for example, Microsoft Exchange) or enterprise database environments (for example, Microsoft SQL Server) on it. VMware made a push to change companies' minds and virtualize these busy servers. VMware made this push in different ways. But the one that counted was making VMware's products better. VMware is now more stable, scalable, and cost-effective. Many companies deploy Exchange and SQL Server, among other business-critical applications, on the VMware virtual platform. And VMware can dynamically scale resources to varying needs on the fly. For example, determining the right-sized physical server for running SQL can be difficult because demands on SQL can change so rapidly. You buy a brand new server to run SQL, and then six months later the physical server is not fast enough. With VMware, you can just increase the amount of memory installed or the number of CPUs. In fact, in some cases you can add memory or CPUs while the server is still running! I don't think you will ever try that with a physical server—at least, not more than once.

This section just scratched the surface of data center virtualization. But grasping the initial concepts is the first step: you should now know why virtualization started, its advantages, and why it is a big deal to companies. Next, we will talk about physical and virtual data center components and differentiating between the two.

Physical and Virtual Data Center Components

This section covers physical and virtual data center components and shows how to differentiate between the two.

Physical Data Center Components

Imagine a large data center in your company. There are many physical servers, each one running an operating system and installed applications. Each physical server has one or more CPUs, memory, storage, and network ports. There are also physical network switches and storage devices. All of these things cost money and consume resources, such as power and cooling, that also cost money.

Physical data center components are physical in the sense that you can touch them. Pretty obvious, I know. However, to understand virtualization, you need to really think about what makes up physical components so it is easier to recognize virtual components and the role they play in the data center. When you open up a physical server, you can examine the hardware devices that make it work. There is a CPU, memory, network cards, and storage. Each of these can be represented by software in a virtual machine.

There are physical boxes in your data center such as servers, network switches, and storage devices. You can think of virtual components in a data center as completely replacing the physical counterparts. So, for example, when you are troubleshooting a virtual network card, you can think of what a physical network card does and expect the same exact properties and functionality in the virtual version.

Virtual Data Center Components

Virtual hardware components are software resources that provide virtual machines with a virtual copy of physical hardware. For example, the network port on a physical computer provides network communication. VMware created a driver for the network card that talks to the hypervisor (ESXi), and that same hypervisor talks to each virtual machine. On the virtual machine end of the hypervisor, everything is digital. There is no need for an actual network cable. A virtual machine running Windows 2012 has a virtual network card constructed of software in the network properties. This is the digital driver that VMware developed.

The ESXi hypervisor talks directly to the physical hardware of the host computer. The ESXi hypervisor also handles any requests from the operating system and installed applications within the virtual machine. The ESXi hypervisor acts as the perfect traffic cop between the physical host computer components and the virtual machine components.

The following are examples of virtual data center components:

- Network interface card
- Memory
- Hard drives
- CPU
- Server
- Network switch
- Network router

Notice that these are exactly the same as the physical devices. That is the point: the same devices providing the same resources, just in software.

On a physical server with an operating system and applications, the operating system handles communication from any installed application to the network card. So if you have a dozen applications installed on a physical computer and all of them want to talk on the network, all of the network requests go to the operating system. And a network driver installed on an operating system further abstracts the physical network card. If you replace the network card on a physical computer with a different card, you will likely have to install a new driver for the network card. The installed applications on the physical server do not know or care that it is a different physical network card that it is talking to.

Some virtual data center components don't have a physical representation. For example:

- Cluster
- Data center
- vApp
- Distributed switch
- vCenter
- Template
- Other VMware appliances

A *cluster* is a group of servers running ESXi. By grouping the servers, you can manage their aggregate resources. If you have 10 physical ESXi hosts with 4 CPUs and 64 GB of memory each, you manage 40 CPUs and 640 GB of memory. VMware's vSphere features such as high availability (HA) and Distributed Resource Scheduler (DRS) work at the cluster level.

A *data center* is a logical grouping of folders and clusters. This logical grouping is used to separate clusters from each other. You can also leverage this for a security boundary. For example, if your company has a separate support group for Windows and Linux, each group can create its own data center.

A *vApp* is a logical way to group applications. Let's say you have 10 web servers running as virtual machines. A vApp allows you to manage them as one. For example, you can shut down the application, and that would shut down all 10 web servers.

Distributed switches are used to connect multiple ESXi hosts together so that the hosts can provide the same network to virtual machines. Distributed switches are more flexible than the standard network virtual switch, often referred to as a *vSwitch*. For example, let's say you have 10 ESXi hosts running virtual machines that are communicating on 10 different subnets. With a standard vSwitch, you have to set up all 10 networks on each host. If you make any mistakes, it can cause problems when you move virtual machines around to different ESXi hosts. When you use a distributed switch, you can configure the 10 networks once, and each host is configured consistently.

vCenter Server is a management application for VMware's vSphere virtual environments that can run as an installed Windows application or a virtual machine running as an appliance. vCenter is a data center component, and it is an important one. vCenter is what ties together all the management aspects of the VMware environment.

A *template* is used to deploy virtual machines. A template is basically a virtual machine configured with an installation of an operating system that you can use to roll out many new virtual machines. You have different templates for different operating systems and configurations. For example, say you have a Linux web server with Apache installed and configured for your organization. You can convert the virtual machine into a template with a mouse click. Then you can just click and deploy new servers, one or a hundred.

Other VMware appliances include solutions such as vRealize Orchestrator and the vSphere Storage Appliance (VSA) that are deployed as a data center component and a virtual appliance.

Physical and Virtual Component Differences

It is easier to understand data center virtualization if you understand data centers in general, even ones not yet virtualized. Data centers can be big or small, but most share the same basic parts. Some virtual hardware components are easier to understand if they have physical counterparts. For example, imagine a network card. You know it plugs into a server and has connections for network cable. Now, imagine a virtual network card. It has the exact same functionality.

Say you have a data center with dozens of racks in rows of servers. Virtualization can convert these rows of racks of servers into just one row of racks. Consolidation not only lets you save money on power and cooling, but it also enables you to buy a smaller data center and save a lot more, or at least have room to grow.

A physical server is basically a system of interconnected hardware devices, rolled up in a neat little package. Examples of hardware devices include CPUs, memory, storage, network ports (embedded or card), and other installed cards. A physical server for a data center is usually a very high-end computer. Of course, servers are expensive and provide redundancy, capacity, and fail-safe solutions built in. A physical server consumes power and gets hot. Each physical server in a data center has an installed operating system with installed applications. When you are talking about the physical computer or server that runs the ESXi hypervisor, that server is often referred to as an ESXi *host.*

 A physical server with a hypervisor installed is referred to as a *host.* Typical vendors are HP and Dell. Physical servers have Intel or AMD processors, memory, network interface cards, and storage.

Routers and switches are hardware devices that provide network packet routing between all of your connected devices. You are using a router when you get on the Internet. A data center can have many routers and switches. Routers and switches also consume power and get hot. Most data centers have some form of cooling to help with the excessive heat generated by all of these devices. With VMware, you can leverage virtualized routers and switches as well.

Shared storage can take many forms. One of the most common in enterprise data centers is fiber attached storage. Shared storage can also be provided by network-attached storage (NAS) devices, and even Network File System (NFS) network volumes. Shared storage is essential for getting the benefits from some virtualization techniques. The hypervisor abstracts storage from the underlying virtual machine, which allows many types of storage devices to be used with the VMware ESXi hypervisor.

 Many kinds of hardware devices can be represented as software in VMware. Hardware devices include network interface cards, hard drives, and CPUs. Hardware devices also can include the physical server as well as routers and switches.

Before virtualization, some companies would load up multiple applications onto each server in order to leverage the existing hardware investment. For example, let's say you have a file server providing data storage to users on your corporate network. However, the server is usually idle and uses only 10 percent of its hardware resources. Now you are asked to install a web server that will have a few demands on the resources. Do you buy a new server to host the web server? You may be tempted to just install the new application on the existing file server to save some money. Many companies did this and experienced problems when one application blew up and took out all applications installed on the same server. Other companies' IT departments knew about the risk of installing many applications on each server. They would just buy another server when a new application was needed. These companies did not experience the problem of one application taking down another because it was installed on the same hardware. However, the hardware costs for these IT departments increased dramatically because of the additional servers they needed to buy. More servers equal more money spent on power and cooling.

If only there were a way to install applications on a server and not have the vulnerability of one application taking down another. This is exactly what virtualization does! You can install a separate operating system to host each application without increasing the number of physical servers you need. This addresses the problem that companies had with having to buy a new physical server every time a new application was rolled out. It also addresses the problem of putting multiple applications on the same physical server.

Virtualization abstracts the operating system and applications from the underlying physical hardware. This abstraction is done by the ESXi hypervisor, which provides everything the physical server provides, but does it in software. The hypervisor is basically a traffic cop that gives each virtual machine access to the hardware when needed. It effectively isolates each virtual machine and allows the underlying hardware to be shared. Since each virtual machine is isolated, one virtual machine will not cause a problem to other virtual machines on the same host.

How Physical to Virtual Machine Conversion Works

Virtualization converts hardware devices into software resources. The virtual machine includes all of the hardware that existed on the physical computer that was virtualized. A VMware program called VMware vCenter Converter does the work of creating a virtual machine based on a physical server.

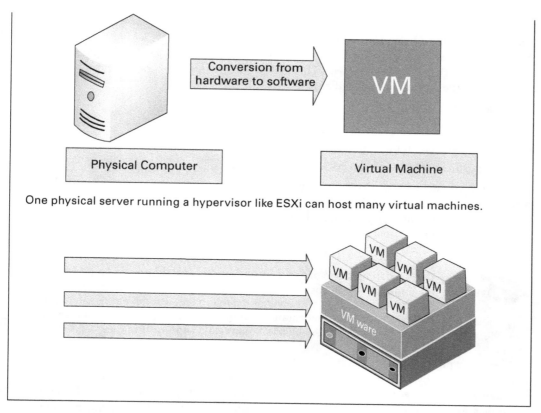

One physical server running a hypervisor like ESXi can host many virtual machines.

After virtualization, one physical computer or ESXi host can host many virtual machines. This is the magic of virtualization. You can now consolidate many physical servers into one. Consolidation is a big deal. Fewer servers means less power used, and less cooling required, which means the potential for massive cost savings. This is the basic reason companies of all sizes are being drawn to virtualization and VMware's solutions. The cheaper your IT is, the more competitive your company can be.

This section provided a basic core understanding of physical and virtual hardware devices. You should know the difference between physical and virtual servers and know that virtualization is the process of converting hardware devices into software resources. You already have a sense of some of the benefits of virtualization, but next we will discuss those in more detail.

Benefits of Using Virtualization

This section covers the benefits of virtualization. We will start by listing some of the biggest challenges many data centers face and then describe how virtualization software mitigates those challenges.

Imagine you are responsible for a large data center. You have over a thousand servers, and each one consumes a hefty amount of power. Each server generates a lot of heat, and heat is bad for server health. A large data center like this would have many switches, routers, and storage devices that also generate heat. This makes cooling the data center critical.

These are the most common challenges:

- Power usage
- Cooling
- Server cost (capital budget)
- Management of physical servers (operational budget)

Power, cooling, and server cost challenges are addressed by consolidation. Consolidation means fewer physical servers. Fewer physical servers directly relates to how much power is used, how much heat is generated, and how much is spent on hardware. The hypervisor makes consolidation a possibility.

Consolidation is one of the biggest benefits of VMware solutions and is leveraged for large cost savings and flexibility. Through consolidation, you save money not only on power and cooling, but also on data center real estate. Data center real estate is a large expense for most companies, and the server sprawl of the '90s left many data centers cramped.

Managing physical computers is easy when you have only one or two. What if you have a hundred? If you have many servers, they may be different makes and models. Managing a lot of servers is no easy task. And when you need to upgrade the hardware on an application server, typically you will have an outage as you reinstall the application on the new server. Now, imagine you still have a hundred servers, but the hardware has been virtualized. Every server can have the same drivers and configuration more easily. And upgrading the hardware can be done with no downtime to the application server. This is a big deal when the application is a critical one!

One other piece of virtualization software that addresses both power usage and cooling, and to a lesser extent, server cost, is Distributed Power Management (DPM), which requires a vCenter server to implement. The basic idea of DPM is to dynamically move all virtual machines from an entire ESXi host and to power down that host.

🌐 Real World Scenario

Leveraging DPM for Profit

Here is one scenario where a company can save a lot of money by leveraging DPM. Let's say you have 1,000 virtual application servers that are very busy during the day running an important application. These virtual machines are hosted on 50 ESXi hosts. In the evening, these are not used at all. By leveraging Distributed Power Management, vCenter can move all these virtual machines to two or three hosts and power down the now unused hosts. This can save the company a lot of cooling and power expenses.

With some of the advanced functionality that VMware provides, you can take this one step further. Let's say you have 100 virtual machines running Windows that are needed only during the day. Let's also say you have 100 virtual machines running Linux but need them only at night. You can automatically decommission the Windows servers every day and deploy Linux as needed, and reverse the process in the morning. That way, you can really limit the number of physical servers you need running the hypervisor. The same hypervisor can run Windows during the day and Linux at night. This kind of setup is advanced but possible because of virtualization. Not that you cannot do the same thing without virtualization, but it is much harder to do without it.

There are many benefits of data center virtualization. The most obvious, and the one that usually gets the attention of management, is reduced cost. Here is a list of benefits to start us off:

- Reduced cooling needs
- Reduced power consumption
- Application isolation
- Fast deployment
- High availability
- Distributed Resource Scheduler
- Configuration management
- Automated workflows

Let's break each of these down.

Reduced Power and Cooling   A great benefit of virtualization is consolidation. Basically, you have fewer physical servers that are hosts to the virtual machines in the data center. Fewer servers means reduced power and cooling requirements.

Application Isolation   Instead of having many applications on a physical computer, after virtualization, each application can have its own operating system and virtual hardware that is isolated from other virtual machines on the same physical host. This isolation provides a separation from other applications and makes for a more robust data center. For example, a web server that crashes will not take down other virtual machines or applications that were installed on the same physical server before the virtualization effort.

Fast Deployment   Before virtualization, getting a new server up and running in a typical data center could take weeks. You would have to order the server, wait for shipment, have the server racked, and get networking and storage configured. Then you'd have to install the operating system, install required software such as antivirus programs, and make configuration changes so that all the physical servers had a consistent configuration. After a data center is virtualized, you can leverage VMware products like vCenter to deploy virtual machines in minutes. The new virtual machines can be completely configured with all required applications installed as well as consistent custom configurations. You use virtual machine templates to realize this benefit.

Using Templates

Templates are used to deploy virtual machines, not physical hosts with a hypervisor like ESXi! A template is a file on the VMware datastore, so deploying a virtual machine from a template requires a file copy to a new datastore location.

High Availability   High availability—often simply referred to as HA—is a fantastic benefit of virtualization that most virtual data centers could not live without. High availability is a service that runs on each physical ESXi host in a cluster, to monitor every other ESXi host in that cluster. If a single ESXi host in a cluster fails, the other hosts in the cluster realize the failure and automatically re-register the virtual machines to other ESXi hosts and then power the virtual machines back up.

Before virtualization, a mad scramble would occur when a server failed. Typically, an engineer would have to replace the failed hardware before bringing the server back online. But what if you had to order the new parts? Suddenly, you would have to waste a lot of time waiting on the postal service. Some companies would buy extra servers just for this reason, which raised the cost of the data center. And if the server failed in the middle of the night, you either would not know until the next morning, or you would have to drive into work in the middle of the night and attempt to repair the server with heavy eyelids.

After virtualization, things got much better. By leveraging high availability, a physical host server could crash—in this case, the ESXi host—and all the virtual machines on that ESXi host would automatically be powered back on after re-registering to a new ESXi host in the cluster. The virtual machines on the failed ESXi host would endure a hard reset, but typically they would be up in running in a short amount of time.

High availability also extends to virtual machines and applications running on virtual machines. HA can restart a virtual machine on a different host—with spare capacity—when the ESXi host it resided on crashes. HA can restart a virtual machine on the same host when the virtual machine's operating system crashes. In addition, HA—with VMware's vFabric Hyperic and vSphere App HA virtual appliances installed—can restart an application service when an issue is detected. HA protects against host failure, virtual machine operating system crashes, and application crashes.

High availability is amazing, and this is one of the first things new VMware deployments can leverage. However, when an ESXi server fails and HA kicks in, the virtual machines on the failed host experience a power outage before other hosts take action and bring the virtual machines back online.

Distributed Resource Scheduler (DRS)   The Distributed Resource Scheduler (DRS) does a good job of spreading workloads across a defined cluster. Some virtual machines use a lot of memory, others use a lot of CPU resources, and it can be a difficult job to spread these uneven loads across multiple physical ESXi hosts. DRS can do this for you, and it can do it on the fly as resource needs change for virtual machines. This is a great benefit.

Configuration Management   When you have hundreds or thousands of servers, maintaining a consistent configuration can be a huge problem. Configuration management tools like vRealize Operations (formerly called VMware Operations Manager) take care of configuration and do a lot more as well. vRealize Operations enables policy-based automation for configuration and security hardening as well as capacity management, application-aware infrastructure management, and performance management.

Automated Workflows   One of the benefits of data center virtualization is scalability. You can use automated workflows to enable VMware to handle a large number of servers. One example is the routine patching of servers. If your company has five web servers handling all of your traffic and you want to update them, you would log into vSphere and snapshot a server before installing the update. You would do each server in turn. But what if you had hundreds of servers? If you use vSphere to do something, you can do the same thing with a workflow. And, if you need to do that "something" to hundreds of virtual machines, it only makes sense to create a workflow to automate it and share it with everyone that needs it. That way, that "something" is done consistently and correctly every time.

Deploying workflows in vSphere uses vRealize Orchestrator. This is a free virtual app that comes with vCenter. Plug-ins for Orchestrator allow you to control many other aspects of your environment. Automated workflows is an advanced topic that is probably not covered on the exam, but it is an interesting feature.

This section talked about the benefits of data center virtualization and hinted at what you can expect, and plan for, when deploying virtualization. Next we will discuss some online tools you can use to further your knowledge about data center virtualization.

Online Tools

This section presents three valuable online tools that are available to you for expanding your knowledge of VMware products. You can use just this book for the test, but you are encouraged to check these out as well. It is always better to overprepare. Future chapters will let you know about additional online resources that can help you study for your test.

The VMware Certified Associate test blueprint calls out three resources for this chapter:

- VMware vSphere Basics Guide
- Virtualization Basics
- VMware Virtualization Toolkit

The VMware vSphere Basics Guide is on VMware's website:

```
https://pubs.vmware.com/vsphere-50/topic/com.vmware.ICbase/PDF/vsphere-
esxi-vcenter-server-50-basics-guide.pdf
```

A quick Google search for *VMware vSphere Basics Guide* may be an easier way to find this online. This guide covers exactly what you think it would: basic information on vSphere that will likely be covered on the exam. If you are just starting to get into virtualization, this is a good place to start.

Virtualization Basics is an online HTML guide:

```
https://www.vmware.com/virtualization/virtualization-basics/what-is-
virtualization.html
```

This guide provides a good overview of virtualization. If you have had exposure to VMware, this resource will make a lot of sense. It offers a good general overview of the topic.

The VMware Virtualization Toolkit provides a lot of information that can be useful when you are just getting into the virtualization game. You do have to register in order to download the toolkit; visit `www.vmware.com/virtualization101_register`. After registering, you will be presented with a web page with links to download white papers, watch videos, read review guides, download a 60-day evaluation of the software, and use a decent online TCO/ROI (total cost of ownership/return on investment) calculator.

The VMware site provides many more resources; these are just a few of the basics. In fact, a section in the appendix will discuss in detail very good online resources to greatly expand your understanding of VMware products.

Summary

This chapter presented a core understanding of data center virtualization and the challenges that it addresses. We talked about how to identify physical and virtual hardware devices. We discussed some of the benefits of data center virtualization and a few online tools.

We started with the basics of data center virtualization. We discussed the physical hardware devices that exist in your data center, such as servers and network switches. We also discussed the power and cooling challenges that physical hardware creates, in addition to capital expenses and management costs. We noted that consolidation goes a long way toward meeting these challenges. Consolidation is the big concept here; one of the biggest advantages is that consolidation is made possible by the VMware hypervisor (ESXi). We also showed that management costs can be addressed in different ways. Consolidation, rapid deployment, high availability, and increased utilization all reduce management costs.

We discussed the benefits of data center virtualization on a deeper level and why server consolidation is such a big deal. You learned that power savings and lower cooling costs as well as capital expenses and management costs are more controllable after virtualization. Finally, we took a look at several online resources that would be beneficial to review for the subjects in this chapter. These valuable resources will help with basic understanding as well as more advanced topics covered later in this book.

Exam Essentials

Be able to explain what data center virtualization is.   Data center virtualization is the conversion of physical hardware devices into software resources. The hypervisor (ESXi) talks directly to the physical hardware, presents virtual copies of hardware to virtual machines, and isolates virtual machines from each other.

Differentiate physical and virtual data center components.   Virtual data center components are software, servers, routers, and switches that can be virtual. Physical data center components are those you can touch, like physical servers, physical switches, and physical routers.

Identify data center virtualization benefits.   Consolidation is one of the biggest benefits of virtualization and means fewer servers, less power, and less cooling are needed. After virtualization, automation is more flexible, management costs are lower, and capital expenditures are lower.

Review Questions

You can find the answers in Appendix A.

1. What is an advantage of data center virtualization?
   - **A.** Less power is consumed.
   - **B.** Fewer physical servers are needed.
   - **C.** It saves money on cooling.
   - **D.** All of the above.

2. What is the best definition of *data center virtualization*?
   - **A.** Conversion of hardware devices into software resources
   - **B.** Management of all servers in the enterprise
   - **C.** Storage vMotion
   - **D.** Existence of vCenter Server

3. How many virtual machines can a physical ESXi host support?
   - **A.** 1
   - **B.** 10 times the number of processors
   - **C.** 100
   - **D.** Many; it depends on the resources provided and needed.

4. What is a hypervisor?
   - **A.** vCenter Server
   - **B.** vRealize Orchestrator
   - **C.** A resource traffic cop
   - **D.** Virtual storage

5. What is the biggest advantage of virtualization?
   - **A.** Using vCenter Server
   - **B.** Load balancing
   - **C.** Server consolidation
   - **D.** Leveraging virtual devices

6. A dozen virtual machines are running on one physical ESXi host after virtualization of your data center. Are the virtual machines aware of each other on this one physical host?
   - **A.** They are aware of each other.
   - **B.** They are aware of each other and can communicate directly.
   - **C.** They are aware of each other and can communicate directly and indirectly.
   - **D.** They are not aware of each other.

7. What is DPM?

   A. Deployment Performance Monitoring

   B. Development Project Management

   C. Distributed Performance Management

   D. Distributed Power Management

8. The physical server with ESXi installed is often referred to as what?

   A. Virtual machine

   B. Host

   C. Server

   D. All of the above

9. VMware supports virtualized versions of what physical devices?

   A. Servers

   B. Servers and routers

   C. Servers, routers, and switches

   D. Servers, routers, switches, and network interface cards

10. A virtual machine running Windows 2012 gets a blue screen of death. What will happen to the other virtual machines on the same ESXi host?

   A. The other virtual machines will be shut down gracefully.

   B. The other virtual machines will be hard-powered off.

   C. The other virtual machines will experience a momentary suspension of computing resources.

   D. Nothing.

11. You can expect to save money on what as a direct result of data center virtualization? (Choose two.)

   A. Management costs

   B. Capital expenses

   C. Windows licenses

   D. Linux licenses

12. Which is the best term to describe reducing the number of physical devices in the data center by virtualization?

   A. Disaster recovery

   B. Archiving

   C. Automation

   D. Consolidation

13. What are the most common challenges addressed by virtualization?

   A. Cooling, consolidation, and conversion

   B. Power usage, cooling, and rack space

   C. Power usage, cooling, and server cost

   D. Power usage, cooling, server cost, and virtual machine management

14. Which VMware component is the hypervisor?

   A. ESXi

   B. vCenter

   C. NSX

   D. Distributed Switch

15. What does the term *consolidation* mean in VMware context?

   A. Converting physical devices to software resources

   B. Storage virtualization

   C. Having fewer physical servers

   D. Capital budget cost savings

16. Which one of these is a benefit of data center virtualization?

   A. More servers

   B. Process speed

   C. Generated heat

   D. Fast server deployment

17. Which of these is a physical hardware device?

   A. Memory

   B. CPU

   C. Network interface card

   D. All of the above

18. What is the resource traffic cop?

   A. vCenter

   B. Storage

   C. Physical CPUs

   D. Hypervisor

19. Which of these are parts of a virtual machine? (Choose three.)

   A. Virtualized operating system

   B. Virtualized applications

   C. Virtualized physical hardware

   D. Virtual switch

20. Which of the following VMware technologies provides virtual copies of server hardware to virtual machines?

   A. vCenter

   B. Hypervisor

   C. Virtual switch

   D. Virtual distributed switch

Chapter

2

VMware Solutions

THE VCA-DCV TOPICS COVERED IN THIS CHAPTER INCLUDE THE FOLLOWING:

✓ **Identify common business challenges addressed by VMware solutions**

   ▪ Identify common availability challenges

   ▪ Identify common management challenges

   ▪ Identify common scalability challenges

   ▪ Identify common optimization challenges

✓ **Apply VMware data center virtualization solutions to common business challenges**

   ▪ Apply VMware data center virtualization technologies to resolve common availability challenges

   ▪ Apply VMware data center virtualization technologies to resolve common management challenges

   ▪ Apply VMware data center virtualization technologies to resolve common optimization challenges

   ▪ Apply VMware data center virtualization technologies to resolve common scalability challenges

This chapter presents common challenges that are faced by businesses and the VMware solutions that can be used to help overcome them. You'll learn about availability challenges, followed by management challenges, scalability challenges, and finally optimization challenges. Once you understand the types of challenges that fall into each category, you will briefly look at the VMware products and technologies that are designed to help mitigate them. Many of these products are described in more detail in later chapters. By the end of this chapter, you will be able to identify common business challenges and recommend a VMware product or technology to help overcome them.

Availability Challenges

Availability challenges consist of anything that can cause an important application to become unavailable to the users who rely on it or that can cause an application outage to go on longer than absolutely necessary. They can range from a single application or server being offline to an entire data center being down because of a large-scale disaster. Availability interruptions can be either planned or unplanned. For example, you might plan to take an application down to perform maintenance on the physical server it resides on. An example of an unplanned availability challenge is a hardware failure that causes a physical server to fail, and thus the application that is running on it to become unavailable.

Many availability issues can be mitigated by configuring additional infrastructure components. For example, Microsoft Clustering can help reduce an application's downtime, and having multiple redundant components in a physical server can reduce the possibility of a single hardware failure taking the server down. Unfortunately, no matter how many safeguards you put in place to reduce downtime, it will still happen. We need to accept that reality, while still taking measures to reduce the chances of downtime occurring and to reduce the length of outages when they do happen.

The following is a sampling of availability challenges:

- The failure of a server component (for example, hard drive, memory, power supply)
- The failure of an entire physical server
- Hardware upgrades
- Hardware maintenance
- The need for certain critical applications to have very little or no downtime
- Application upgrades and patching that may cause an application to become unavailable

- A disaster that causes an entire data center to fail
- The ability to test a disaster-recovery scenario without taking down the production data center
- The requirement to have good testable backups

Now that you understand the types of issues that are considered availability challenges, let's look at the VMware products and technologies that can help mitigate them.

VMware Availability Products and Technologies

This section introduces the VMware products and technologies that are designed to help mitigate common availability challenges. This section will not make you an expert on any of these technologies but will give you a basic understanding of what each technology does. You'll learn to identify the products for the exam as well as determine which products you may want to look into further for deploying in your environment.

In this section, you will look at the following VMware availability products and technologies:

- vMotion
- Storage vMotion
- vSphere Data Protection
- vSphere Replication
- Fault tolerance (FT)
- High availability (HA)
- Site Recovery Manager (SRM)
- Virtual machine snapshots

vMotion

vMotion enables running virtual machines to be migrated from one ESXi host to another without experiencing any downtime. In order for vMotion to work correctly, both ESXi hosts must be connected to the same shared storage and must share common networking. vMotion helps mitigate the availability challenges that arise from performing hardware maintenance and upgrades on ESXi hosts as well as from periodically applying patches to ESXi hosts.

vMotion has many uses. It can be used to migrate all the virtual machines off an ESXi host so that hardware maintenance can be performed on it or so that patches can be applied to it. vMotion can also be used to manually move virtual machines from one ESXi host to another in order to more evenly balance the virtual machine workloads across available hosts. It is also used by the Distributed Resource Scheduler to automatically balance virtual machine workloads across available hosts. Finally, vMotion can be used in troubleshooting. By moving a virtual machine from one host to another, you can see whether issues on the virtual machine continue after it is running on the new host. If the issues follow the virtual machine, they most likely are not being caused by any type of hardware problem (because the virtual machines are then running on different hardware).

Storage vMotion

Storage vMotion (svMotion) enables running virtual machines to be migrated from one datastore to another without experiencing any downtime. In order for Storage vMotion to work correctly, both datastores must be accessible by the ESXi host on which the virtual machine resides. Storage vMotion is very much like vMotion and is used to resolve the same types of availability challenges, except it operates on datastores instead of hosts. Storage vMotion can be used to resolve the availability challenges that arise from performing maintenance on datastores and moving virtual machines from older datastores to new datastores during storage upgrades.

The best way to think of Storage vMotion is to look at it as vMotion that works on datastores instead of ESXi hosts. The most common use for Storage vMotion is to move a virtual machine drive to another datastore so it can be expanded, or to free up space on the original datastore for another virtual machine's drives to be extended. It can also be used to migrate virtual machines off a datastore so maintenance can be performed on the datastore or it can be decommissioned. In the same way that DRS uses vMotion to distribute virtual machine workloads across hosts, Storage Distributed Resource Scheduler - RMS (SDRS) uses svMotion to distribute storage workloads across available datastores.

vSphere Data Protection

vSphere Data Protection is a VMware solution for backing up and restoring virtual machines. Because vSphere Data Protection creates a backup of the entire virtual machine, performing virtual machine restores using vSphere Data Protection is much easier than with more-traditional file-backup methods. The backups that are created by vSphere Data Protection are fully testable, and restores can be performed on individual files or entire virtual machines as needed. vSphere Data Protection can help ensure that you have good testable backups and are protected against a disaster that causes an entire data center to fail. Even if you are using full-scale disaster-recovery packages, you can easily find yourself relying on your backups to help restore some of your servers in a disaster.

vSphere Replication

vSphere Replication is a hardware-independent technology that allows running virtual machines to be replicated to another site. If a disaster occurs at the original site, the replica virtual machine can be brought up at the other site. Unlike with more-advanced disaster-recovery solutions, the target virtual machine is not automatically brought online, and an application outage occurs when the original server fails, until the replicated server is brought online by an administrator. vSphere Replication is primarily used to add another layer of protection to a critical server that may need to be quickly brought up at an alternate site. This technology can help recover from the failure of an entire physical server or, to a limited degree, the failure of an entire data center.

Fault Tolerance

Fault tolerance (FT) enables a mirror to be created of a virtual machine. As changes are made to the original virtual machine, they are also made to the mirror. If the original virtual machine fails, the mirror takes over without any application downtime.

The best use for fault tolerance is to mirror virtual machines that are running critical applications and require nearly zero downtime. Because FT is easy to configure and manage, it can be useful for applications that may not be critical but would be problematic if they failed. The availability challenge that is covered by FT is the need for certain critical applications to have very little or no downtime. In the real world, nothing can guarantee zero downtime, but FT can greatly reduce downtime occurrences.

Many of the technologies that promise zero downtime have issues, and some can even cause more problems than they solve. When I first heard about fault tolerance, I thought it would have issues that would make it less than useful. Once I started testing it, though, I was pleasantly surprised. Fault tolerance is easy to set up and appears to work as promised.

High Availability

High availability (HA) is used to automatically restart virtual machines on a different ESXi host if the ESXi host they are on fails. Even though the virtual machines experience an outage while being restarted, it is a much shorter outage than if the machines had to be manually restarted. This can be extremely important if an ESXi host fails in the middle of the night when no administrators are available. The challenge that is resolved by HA is the failure of an entire physical server.

Before HA was available, the failure of a single ESXi host meant that a large number of virtual machines that were running on it would be down. This was referred to as the "all of your eggs in one basket" issue and caused some companies not to deploy virtual servers. Deploying HA negated this issue, and companies felt better about deploying large numbers of virtual machines on their ESXi hosts.

A nice feature of HA is that it allows you to configure a restart order for your virtual machines. Some virtual machines require that other virtual machines be up and running before they are booted. The restart order allows you to restart the virtual machines in a specified order so that these types of dependencies can be met.

Advantages of HA and FT over Other Cluster Technologies

I have worked at many large technology companies whose clients need 24-hour access to their applications, with very minimal downtime. Various options can be used to provide minimal application downtime, such as redundant load-balanced applications running on separate hardware, or application-clustering solutions like Microsoft Clustering. All of these solutions have their advantages and disadvantages, but they all tend to be expensive and difficult to set up correctly.

Now that most of my clients' environments have been virtualized, I can use VMware solutions to help resolve the issue of minimal downtime. I use HA for applications that need to have very low downtime, and FT for those that need near-zero downtime. Compared to the other solutions I have tried, HA and FT are extremely easy to get up and running and are already available in the client's environment. The combination of HA and FT has greatly reduced the application downtime for many of my clients.

Site Recovery Manager

Site Recovery Manager (SRM) is a VMware disaster-recovery solution that can restore an entire data center with the press of a few buttons. During the configuration of SRM, detailed disaster-recovery plans are developed that are used by the package to fully restore business operations at an alternate site in the event of a full-scale disaster. SRM, which is relatively straightforward to configure, makes it easy to initiate a recovery. The availability challenges resolved by SRM include the failure of an entire data center from a disaster and the ability to test a disaster-recovery scenario without taking down the production data center.

An important feature of Site Recovery Manager is that it allows any part of the disaster-recovery plan, or the entire plan, to be fully tested while the production systems are still online. This testing is key because it can help you discover any issues with your plan and correct them before a real disaster occurs. Unfortunately, many companies find out that their disaster-recovery plans are incomplete while they are trying to recover from a disaster. This can cause recovery from a disaster to take longer and in some cases to be impossible.

Virtual Machine Snapshots

Virtual machine snapshots enable an administrator to create a point-in-time recovery point for a virtual machine. If a snapshot has been taken of a virtual machine and that virtual machine later fails, it can quickly be reverted to the state it was in when the snapshot was taken. Virtual machine snapshots are used mainly to protect against failures that are caused by applying operating system and application patches or upgrades.

To successfully use virtual machine snapshots, they must be taken before any changes are made to the virtual machine. After the snapshot has been taken, the patch or upgrade can be applied to the virtual machine. Then the virtual machine must be monitored for a period of time. If issues are experienced on the virtual machine, you can easily revert it to the state it was in when the snapshot was taken. If no issues are experienced, the snapshot can be deleted. Snapshots do use space, so they should be deleted after a reasonable amount of time has passed.

Virtual machine snapshots can be extremely useful when performing operating system patches. Everyone assumes that patches have been fully tested by the vendor and should not cause any issues when they are applied. Unfortunately, this is not always the case. Before I apply an operating system patch, I always create a snapshot of the virtual machine. This adds a little time to the patching process, but it has saved me several times when the patches caused the system to become unstable. Because I had a snapshot, I was able to quickly revert the server to the state it was in before the patches were applied.

Now that we have identified the availability challenges that companies experience and you have a basic understanding of the VMware products and technologies that can help mitigate them, we will move on to management challenges.

Management Challenges

Management challenges cause your infrastructure to become more unwieldy as it continues to grow and age. You might, for example, need to provide centralized tools to manage and control the infrastructure. Issues might arise related to compliance and the need to keep the infrastructure modern. As many infrastructures grow, the management tools that were effective when the system was smaller are not able to keep up with the growth. Some infrastructures may also be encumbered by the limitations of having older hardware mixed in with newer, more powerful hardware. These inconsistencies in the environment can become difficult to manage.

The following are examples of management challenges:

- Centralized management of the environment
- Replacement of out-of-date or unsupported hardware
- Compliance monitoring of the environment

Now that you understand the types of issues that are considered management challenges, let's look at the VMware products and technologies that can help mitigate them.

VMware Management Products and Technologies

This section describes the VMware products and technologies that are designed to meet common management challenges. Like the preceding section, this one will not make you an expert on any of these technologies. It will give you a basic understanding of what each technology does and the capability to identify uses for the products, which is required for the exam. This section will also help you determine which products you may want to consider deploying in your environment.

In this section, you will look at the following VMware management products and technologies:

- Virtual machines
- vCenter Server
- vCenter Configuration Manager

Virtual Machines

Virtual machines (VMs) are essentially physical servers that are completely represented in software. They have all the advantages of physical servers without many of the disadvantages. The two main uses for virtual machines are to replace existing physical servers and to deploy new servers without deploying large numbers of new physical servers. Because VMs do not have physical hardware, they can help meet the management challenge of needing to replace out-of-date or unsupported hardware.

Physical servers can be replaced by virtual machines by using a process called *physical-to-virtual (P2V) conversions*. This process allows all the applications and settings from an existing physical server to be converted onto a new virtual server. Once the process has been completed, the older physical server is powered off and decommissioned while the new virtual server is powered on. The new virtual server will perform just like the original physical server.

New virtual machines can be quickly created and deployed in a number of ways that will be discussed later in this chapter. The best way to think of a virtual machine is that it can do anything a physical server can do and then some. Virtual machines are the main component of any virtual environment.

vCenter Server

vCenter Server is a centralized management tool for VMware vSphere environments. It provides a single pane through which most of the vSphere environment is controlled. The vast majority of the features we discuss in this book are accessed through a client connected to vCenter Server. Many of the other features in a VMware infrastructure depend on vCenter Server to function. vCenter Server has an open architecture, so many vendors that are creating features for vSphere integrate them into vCenter Server.

vCenter Configuration Manager

vCenter Configuration Manager (VCCM) is a powerful VMware solution for tracking, reporting, and alerting on configuration changes in the virtual environment. It allows configuration baselines to be created for the virtual servers and then tracks against the baselines any changes that are made. It can be used to quickly and accurately generate configuration change reports that can be certified and turned into regulators. VCCM can help remediate the management challenge of needing accurate compliance monitoring of the virtual environment. VCCM is in the process of being included into a new product named vRealize Operations, but the term *vCenter Configuration Manager* appears on the current exam.

Scalability Challenges

Scalability challenges cause issues as a company's infrastructure continues to grow or limit a company's ability to quickly meet new challenges. Processes and tools that worked well for a smaller environment often are no longer sufficient as the environment grows. The process of installing an operating system by putting a CD into a physical server and manually installing it may be OK if your environment has a few servers, but is no longer efficient when you have hundreds or even thousands of servers.

Companies are becoming more and more dependent on technology infrastructures and are expecting them to be more responsive. In the past, it may have been all right that a request for a new server to host an application would take several weeks to be online. That kind of required lead time is no longer acceptable in many organizations, and it is just expected that new servers can be quickly rolled out. These types of delays can cost a company revenue due to lost opportunities.

The following are examples of scalability challenges:

- Application isolation
- Load balancing server workloads
- Load balancing storage workloads
- The ability to quickly deploy new servers
- The ability to use features that require shared storage at branch offices
- The ability to upgrade server resources without an application outage

Now that you understand the types of issues that are considered scalability challenges, let's look at the VMware products and technologies that can be used to meet them.

VMware Scalability Products and Technologies

This section describes the VMware products and technologies that are designed to help mitigate common scalability challenges. You will briefly look at the capabilities of each product and identify uses for them. You will learn enough details to be able to identify each product on the exam. Hopefully, this information will encourage you to look deeper at the products you feel would be useful in your environment.

In this section, you will look at the following VMware scalability products and technologies:

- Virtual machines
- Virtual machine templates
- Distributed Resource Scheduler (DRS)
- Storage DRS
- vSphere Storage Appliance (VSA)
- Hot add

Virtual Machines

As stated earlier, virtual machines (VMs) are physical servers that are completely represented in software. Many VMs can run on a single physical server called a *host*. Virtual machines essentially replace the need for physical application servers and have a number of advantages over physical servers. Since adding additional virtual machines does not add additional hardware costs, a new virtual machine can be deployed for each application that is running in the environment. By having only one application running on each virtual machine, you can achieve total application isolation. When you have multiple applications running on a single server, the failure of one application can often cause other applications to fail and possibly cause the entire server to fail. You can also experience issues when one application needs to be upgraded and requires the server to be restarted. If you have multiple applications running on the server, all of them will need to be taken down when the server is rebooted.

Another advantage of virtual machines over physical servers is that they can be deployed very quickly. In a typical physical environment, it can take weeks to deploy a new physical server from the time it is ordered until it is ready to be used. In a properly configured virtual environment, new virtual servers can be deployed in a matter of hours, and if you are deploying very similar servers, many of them can be deployed very quickly.

Virtual Machine Templates

You can convert a fully configured virtual machine into a *virtual machine template*, which can then be used to rapidly deploy large numbers of new virtual machines that are configured like the original virtual machine. Using templates has a couple of significant advantages over manually creating new virtual machines: when using templates, you do not need to repeatedly install software that is on every virtual machine, such as antivirus packages and backup software. You also have a reduced chance of misconfiguring any software on an individual virtual machine that can be introduced when manually installing packages. Virtual machine templates can mitigate the scalability challenge of quickly deploying new virtual servers.

The process of using virtual machine templates begins with creating a fully configured model virtual machine. This virtual machine should be fully patched and have all of its applications installed. You convert this model to a template by using vCenter Server. Using this template, you can deploy large numbers of similarly configured virtual machines in a matter of minutes. These new virtual machines will look very much like the template but will have their own names and IP addresses. They will also have all of the applications, patches, and configurations as the model virtual machine.

Distributed Resource Scheduler

The *Distributed Resource Scheduler (DRS)* is a VMware technology that load balances virtual machine workloads across ESXi hosts to remove the problem of hot spots, whereby one ESXi host is overused while others go underused. The uneven distribution of virtual machine workloads can cause some of the virtual machines to experience performance issues. The DRS continuously monitors hosts in the cluster and periodically uses vMotion to move virtual machines between the hosts to better balance the virtual machine workloads. The Distributed Resource Scheduler is also used to place new virtual machines onto the least used hosts in the cluster when they are deployed.

Storage DRS

Storage DRS (SDRS) is a VMware technology that load balances virtual machines across datastores. If the virtual machines are not correctly load balanced, the demand on one datastore can be very high while other datastores are underutilized. This can cause the virtual machines running on the overutilized datastore to experience performance issues. By evenly distributing the storage workloads across the available datastores, the virtual machines will not experience storage bottlenecks. Another use for Storage DRS is in the placement of new virtual machines. When a new virtual machine is created, Storage DRS places its drives onto the least heavily used datastore. To move virtual machines from one datastore to another, SDRS uses Storage vMotion.

VSphere Storage Appliance

The *vSphere Storage Appliance (VSA)* is a VMware technology that can be used to aggregate unused disks on ESXi hosts and use them as shared storage. Many smaller companies cannot afford the expense of shared storage, and many larger companies have branch offices where it would not be cost-effective to have shared storage. These companies can use the VSA to take advantage of the storage they already have available in their ESXi hosts to enjoy the benefits of shared storage. Many VMware technologies require shared storage, and the VSA can enable smaller organizations and branch offices to use them. The vSphere Storage Appliance is easy to install and can be up and running in a matter of a few hours.

Hot Add

Hot add is a VMware technology that allows CPU and memory resources to be added to a running virtual machine without incurring downtime. The only condition for using hot add is that the operating system of the virtual machine must be compatible with adding resources. Most modern server operating systems are compatible. Hot add can be extremely useful when applications grow beyond the current configuration of the virtual machine they are running on but must not be taken down for upgrades. Hot add enables companies to meet the scalability challenge of upgrading server resources without incurring an application outage.

Optimization Challenges

Optimization challenges cause applications to run at less-than-peak performance or cause resources to be wasted. Optimization challenges range from performance bottlenecks that are causing applications to be less responsive, to servers that have more resources than they need and are therefore costing the company more than they should. They also include applications that appear to be working correctly but could be performing better if available technologies were implemented. In modern computer environments, it is no longer acceptable to have applications that are not performing as well as they could or that are wasting resources that could be used elsewhere.

The following are examples of optimization challenges:

- Locating performance-based bottlenecks
- Identifying servers that have more resources than they need and "right-sizing" them
- Reclaiming unused storage that has been allocated
- Ensuring that virtual machines are running on the required storage class
- Prioritizing the network traffic of certain virtual machines
- Reducing power usage whenever possible
- Prioritizing storage throughput for certain virtual machines
- Optimizing the performance of virtual machine memory

Right-sizing is the process of reconfiguring existing virtual machines to have the proper amount of CPU and memory resources. It can be difficult to determine the resource requirements of a virtual machine before it is in use, and they are often overallocated. Right-sizing involves monitoring virtual machines over time to see how much memory and CPU they actually use and reconfiguring them to have the proper resources assigned. Periodically performing right-sizing can free up resources for use on other virtual machines and can improve the performance of existing virtual machines.

Next we'll look at the VMware products and technologies that can help address these challenges.

VMware Optimization Products and Technologies

This section presents the VMware products and technologies that are designed to help mitigate common optimization challenges. It will give you enough detail about each product to be able to identify it on the exam and hopefully encourage you to look deeper at the products you feel would be useful in your environment.

In this section, you will look at the following VMware optimization products and technologies:

- vCenter Operations Manager (vCOps)
- Thin provisioning
- VM storage profiles
- Distributed Switch with QoS
- Distributed Power Management (DPM)
- Storage I/O Control (SIOC)
- vFlash

vCenter Operations Manager

vCenter Operations Manager (vCOps) is a VMware product that can actively monitor the virtual environment and find performance bottlenecks. It can also track how virtual machines utilize the resources they have been assigned. This can make it useful for identifying performance issues and for right-sizing virtual machines to regain unused resources.

vCenter Operations Manager is in the process of being included into a new product named vRealize Operations, but *vCenter Operations Manager* is the term that appears on the current exam as of this book's writing.

vCenter Operations Manager can be extremely useful for identifying performance bottlenecks. By keeping track of performance metrics for all the objects in the virtual environment and presenting them as graphs, vCOps makes it easy to see when performance issues started and which virtual object is having an issue. It also keeps resource utilization metrics for all the virtual machines in the environment. This type of data is critical when performing virtual machine right-sizing.

Thin Provisioning

Thin provisioning allows a virtual machine to save drive space by taking up only the space it actually uses. Thin-provisioned drives can grow as they need space, up to a maximum size that is defined by the administrator. Thin provisioning can greatly increase the number of virtual machines that can be placed on a storage array. However, because the storage is overprovisioned, it must be watched carefully to make sure the storage array doesn't become completely full. New virtual machines can be deployed with thin-provisioned disks to guarantee that they will not contain unused space. Existing virtual machines can be converted from standard, thick-provisioned drives to thin-provisioned drives to reclaim any unused space.

VM Storage Profiles

VM storage profiles allow datastores to be separated into performance classes depending on the performance characteristics of the datastore. VM storage profiles are then able to automatically use Storage vMotion to move virtual machine disks to the performance class of datastore on which the virtual machine would perform best. VM storage profiles can be useful for large companies that have many storage solutions with varying performance characteristics. Since higher-performance storage usually costs more than lower-performance storage, money can be saved by having virtual machines running on datastores that have the minimum performance characteristics they need.

Distributed Switch with QoS

Distributed Switch with QoS is a VMware technology that allows the network traffic of certain virtual machines to be prioritized. *QoS*, or *quality of service*, guarantees transmission rates for a given port on the switch. This can be useful when a single virtual machine needs to have greater network access than the others on the same distributed switch. A good use for distributed switches with QoS is a virtual machine that is running streaming video or music applications, since it can have a guaranteed transmission rate.

Distributed Power Management

Distributed Power Management (DPM) is a VMware technology that can save energy by shutting down ESXi hosts when virtual machine workloads are light. DPM continuously monitors virtual machine workloads on all the ESXi hosts in a cluster. When it determines that the workloads are low enough to shut down a host, DPM uses vMotion to move all the virtual machines off the ESXi host and then powers it down. When DPM determines that the virtual machine workload has increased enough that another host is needed, DPM uses wake-on-LAN or IPMI to power on a new host. If a company's virtual machine workloads meet the pattern of higher use during parts of the day and lower use during other parts of the day, implementing DPM can significantly reduce power usage. Distributed Power Management would not be a good fit for a company that has a fairly constant virtual machine workload all of the time.

WARNING   Distributed Power Management can save companies significant costs associated with running servers and cooling data centers, but it does come with some risks. The majority of hardware issues on servers occur when they are rebooted or powered on. Because DPM routinely powers servers off and back on, you could see an increase in the number of failed server components when using it.

Storage I/O Control

Storage I/O Control (SIOC) allows the storage traffic of individual virtual machines to be prioritized over other virtual machines. SIOC can be used to give a single virtual machine greater access to storage resources than other virtual machines located on the same datastore. A good usage case for Storage I/O Control is a critical database server that continuously accesses its storage to update tables. SIOC can enable a company to remediate the optimization challenge of prioritizing storage throughput for certain virtual machines.

vFlash

vFlash allows virtual machines to use solid-state drives on the ESXi host as their cache to increase performance and run optimally. vFlash can optimize the performance of virtual machine memory by redirecting any memory caching that is occurring from slower disks to the solid-state drives. Since the solid-state drive is faster than regular disk, the impact of caching is greatly reduced. vFlash should *not* be used to replace memory upgrades on servers that are caching often but can be useful for those that are caching only occasionally and can accept a small performance hit when the caching occurs.

Key Terms for the Exam

The following are key terms that you should watch for when taking the exam. The highlighted technology is the possible answer when you see the terms below it within the exam question. We've indicated which terms point toward which topics as the answer.

vMotion
- Migrate virtual machines between hosts
- No downtime

Storage vMotion
- Migrate virtual machines between storage locations
- No downtime

vSphere Data Protection
- Backup
- Restore

vSphere Replication
- Replicated
- Remote site
- Backup site

Fault tolerance

- Zero downtime

- Virtual machine mirror

High availability

- Failed ESXi host

- Virtual machine restart

Site Recovery Manager

- Disaster recovery

Virtual machine snapshots

- Point-in-time

- Revert

- Application upgrade

- Patch

Virtual machines

- Physical-to-virtual (P2V)

- Application isolation

vCenter Server

- Management

vCenter Configuration Manager

- Compliance

- Configuration

- Alerting

Virtual machine templates

- Rapid deployment

- Consistent configurations

Distributed Resource Scheduler

- Load balance virtual machine workloads

- Distribute virtual machine workloads

Storage DRS

- Load balance storage workloads

- Distribute storage workloads

vSphere Storage Appliance

- Shared storage

- Branch office

Hot add

- On-the-fly upgrade

- No downtime

- Critical application

vCenter Operations Manager

- Bottleneck

- Right-sizing

- Active monitoring

Thin provisioning

- Overprovisioned

- Unused drive space

- Grow

VM storage profiles

- Storage performance

- Storage class

Distributed Switch with QoS

- Network priority

- Prioritize

- Distributed switch

Distributed Power Management

- Reduce power consumption

- Wake-on-LAN

- IPMI

Storage I/O Control	**vFlash**
▪ Storage priority	▪ Flash memory
▪ Prioritize	▪ Solid-state drives

Note: vMotion, high availability, virtual machines, vCenter Server, and vCenter Operations Manager are examined in more detail in Chapter 3, "vSphere Core Components." Storage vMotion and Storage DRS, vSphere Storage Appliance, thin provisioning, VM storage profiles, and Storage I/O Control are examined in depth in Chapter 4, "Storage in a VMware Environment." We discuss distributed switches with QoS in Chapter 5, "Networking in a VMware Environment."

Summary

In this chapter, we discussed the types of common challenges that businesses face and some of the VMware products and technologies that can be used to mitigate them.

We started by looking at availability challenges such as hardware failures and the need to perform hardware upgrades and maintenance and to have good testable backups. We discussed the need for some applications to have very little or no downtime, the possibility of failed application upgrades causing extended outages, and the need for a testable disaster-recovery solution. We also briefly looked at the following VMware products and technologies that can be used to mitigate availability challenges: vMotion, Storage vMotion, vSphere Data Protection, vSphere Replication, fault tolerance, high availability, Site Recovery Manager, and virtual machine snapshots.

We then moved on to look at the common management challenges that businesses face. These included the need for centralized management of technology infrastructures and the need for compliance monitoring of environments in regulated industries. We discussed the need for virtualizations to efficiently replace out-of-date or unsupported hardware. We briefly looked at the following VMware products and technologies that can be used to mitigate management challenges: virtual machines, vCenter Server, and vCenter Configuration Manager.

Next we examined the scalability challenges that are faced by growing companies. We discussed the need for application isolation and the need to quickly deploy new servers and applications. We also discussed the need to load balance server workloads across physical servers and to balance storage workloads across storage arrays, as well as being able to use the same features at branch offices as are available at the main office. We briefly looked at the following VMware products and technologies that can be used to mitigate scalability challenges: virtual machines, virtual machine templates, Distributed Resource Scheduler, Storage DRS, the vSphere Storage Appliance, and the hot add feature of virtual machines.

Finally, we looked at the common optimization challenges that businesses encounter: locating performance bottlenecks, reclaiming unused storage, and ensuring that servers are located on their proper storage class. We also discussed the need to prioritize network traffic and storage traffic for certain virtual machines. Last we discussed the need to reduce total power usage and optimize virtual machine memory. We briefly looked at the following VMware products and technologies that can be used to mitigate optimization challenges: vCenter Operations Manager, thin provisioning, VM storage profiles, Distributed Switch with QoS, Distributed Power Management, Storage I/O Control, and vFlash.

Exam Essentials

Understand availability challenges. Availability challenges can cause an important application to become unavailable to the users who rely on it or can cause an outage to go on longer than absolutely necessary.

Be able to identify an availability challenge. The following are examples of availability challenges: hardware failures, disasters that cause a data center failure, power outages, application upgrades and patching that cause an application to become unavailable, hardware maintenance, the need for zero downtime, and the requirement to have good testable backups.

Know which VMware technologies can be used to mitigate availability challenges. The following technologies can be used to mitigate many availability challenges: high availability, Site Recovery Manager, vSphere Replication, vMotion, Storage vMotion, snapshots, fault tolerance, and vSphere Data Protection.

Understand management challenges. Management challenges can cause an environment to become harder to manage and understand.

Be able to identify a management challenge. The following issues are examples of management challenges: the need for centralized management of the environment, the need to replace out-of-date or unsupported hardware, and the requirement for compliance monitoring of the environment.

Know which VMware technologies can be used to mitigate management challenges. The following technologies can be used to mitigate many management challenges: virtual machines, vCenter Server, and vCenter Configuration Manager.

Understand scalability challenges. Scalability challenges can cause issues as a company's infrastructure continues to grow or can limit the company's ability to quickly meet new challenges.

Be able to identify a scalability challenge. The following are examples of scalability challenges: application isolation, the need to load balance server and storage workloads, the need to quickly deploy new servers, and the ability to use features that require shared storage at branch offices.

Know which VMware technologies can be used to mitigate scalability challenges. The following technologies can be used to mitigate many scalability challenges: virtual machines, Distributed Resource Scheduler, Storage DRS, virtual machine templates, the vSphere Storage Appliance, and hot add.

Understand optimization challenges. Optimization challenges can cause applications to run at less-than-peak performance or can cause resources to be wasted.

Be able to identify an optimization challenge. The following issues are examples of optimization challenges: locating performance bottlenecks, reclaiming unused storage, ensuring that virtual machines are running on the required storage class, prioritizing the network traffic of virtual machines, reducing power usage whenever possible, prioritizing storage throughput for virtual machines, and optimizing the performance of virtual machine memory.

Know which VMware technologies can be used to mitigate optimization challenges. The following technologies can be used to mitigate many optimization challenges: vCenter Operations Manager, VM storage profiles, Distributed Switch with QoS, Distributed Power Management, Storage I/O Control, and vFlash.

Review Questions

You can find the answers in Appendix A.

1. Which one of the following is an availability challenge?

    A. A physical server failure

    B. The desire to reduce power usage whenever possible

    C. The need to rapidly add new servers

    D. The need to reclaim unused server storage

2. Which VMware technology allows virtual machines to use only the amount of disk space they need, even if they have additional disk space assigned to them?

    A. Storage I/O Control

    B. Thin provisioning

    C. VM storage profiles

    D. vSphere Storage Appliance (VSA)

3. Which VMware technology can be used to give one virtual machine greater access to its storage than other virtual machines located on the same storage?

    A. Distributed Resource Scheduling (DRS)

    B. High availability

    C. Storage DRS (SDRS)

    D. Storage I/O Control (SIOC)

4. Which one of the following is a management challenge?

    A. Replacing outdated or unsupported hardware

    B. The ability to quickly deploy new servers

    C. The need to load balance server workloads

    D. The requirements of very high uptime servers

5. Which VMware technology can be used to reduce the tendency of administrators to place multiple applications onto one server in order to reduce the number of physical servers in a data center?

    A. Fault tolerance

    B. Templates

    C. Virtual machines

    D. vSphere Replication

6. Which one of the following is a scalability challenge?

    A. A physical server failure

    B. The desire to reduce power usage whenever possible

    C. The need to rapidly add new servers

    D. The need to reclaim unused server storage

7. Which of the following best describes fault tolerance?

   A. A hardware-independent solution to replicate a virtual machine or group of virtual machines to another site

   B. A VMware backup solution that allows virtual machines to be easily backed up and restored

   C. A VMware solution that allows two virtual machines to act together for zero downtime in the event one of them fails

   D. A VMware solution that allows a virtual machine to restart on a different host if the host it is running on fails

8. Which VMware technology can help an administrator reduce the risks associated with patching or upgrading applications to newer versions?

   A. Hot add

   B. Snapshots

   C. Templates

   D. vCenter Configuration Manager

9. Which of the following best describes VMware hot-add technology?

   A. The ability to add a second server to a fault-tolerant set without the need for reboots

   B. The ability to add resources such as CPU and memory to compatible virtual machines without the need for a reboot

   C. The ability to rapidly add new virtual machines by using templates

   D. The ability to replicate a virtual machine at another site

10. Which of the following VMware products allows an administrator to use the local drives on ESXi hosts as shared storage?

   A. Storage I/O Control

   B. Thin provisioning

   C. VM storage profiles

   D. vSphere Storage Appliance

11. Which of the following are optimization challenges? (Choose two.)

   A. A physical server failure

   B. The desire to reduce power usage whenever possible

   C. The need to rapidly add new servers

   D. The need to reclaim unused server storage

12. Which VMware technology can be used to migrate a virtual machine from one shared storage location to another while keeping it on the same ESXi host?

   A. Distributed Resource Scheduler (DRS)

   B. Storage vMotion

   C. vMotion

   D. vSphere Replication

13. Which of the following best describes VMware vMotion technology?

    A. The ability to move a running virtual machine from one ESXi host to another with minimal downtime

    B. The ability to move a running virtual machine from one ESXi host to another with no downtime

    C. The ability to move a virtual machine from its current storage array to another storage array with minimal downtime

    D. The ability to move a virtual machine from its current storage array to another storage array with no downtime

14. Which of the following best describes vSphere Data Protection?

    A. A hardware-independent solution to replicate a virtual machine or group of virtual machines to another site

    B. A VMware backup solution that allows virtual machines to be easily backed up and restored

    C. A VMware solution that allows two virtual machines to act together for zero downtime in the event one of them fails

    D. A VMware solution that allows a virtual machine to restart on a different host if the host it is running on fails

15. Which VMware technology helps administrators deploy large numbers of similarly configured virtual machines?

    A. Hot add

    B. Snapshots

    C. Templates

    D. vCenter Configuration Manager

16. Which of the following statements about VMware high availability is not true? (Choose one.)

    A. HA can be used to reduce downtime for virtual machines in the event of a host failure.

    B. HA is used to restart virtual machines on another host when the host they are running on fails.

    C. HA uses vMotion to move virtual machines from the host they are running on to a different host.

    D. When an HA event occurs, the virtual machines running on it experience an outage.

17. Which of the following best describes Storage DRS?

    A. A VMware technology that allows a virtual machine to save space by using only the storage it needs and allows it to expand as its needs increase

    B. A VMware technology that allows the unused drives on ESXi hosts to be used as shared storage

    C. A VMware technology that allows virtual machine workloads to be distributed across multiple storage arrays with minimal downtime

    D. A VMware technology that allows virtual machine workloads to be distributed across multiple storage arrays with no downtime

18. Which of the following VMware technologies can move virtual machines off ESXi hosts and power them off during periods of low utilization and power them back on when utilization picks back up?

   A. Distributed Power Management

   B. Distributed Resource Scheduler

   C. Site Recovery Manager

   D. vCenter

19. Which of the following VMware technologies allows an existing virtual machine to be mirrored by a second virtual machine that can take over in the event that the original virtual machine fails with no application downtime?

   A. Fault tolerance

   B. High availability

   C. Snapshots

   D. vSphere Replication

20. Which of the following best describes high availability?

   A. A hardware-independent solution to replicate a virtual machine or group of virtual machines to another site

   B. A VMware backup solution that allows virtual machines to be easily backed up and restored

   C. A VMware solution that allows two virtual machines to act together for zero downtime in the event one of them fails

   D. A VMware solution that allows a virtual machine to restart on a different ESXi host if the ESXi host it is running on fails

Chapter

3

vSphere Core Components

THE VCA-DCV TOPICS COVERED IN THIS CHAPTER INCLUDE THE FOLLOWING:

✓ **Identify vSphere core components**

  ▪ Explain the concept and capabilities of a virtual machine

  ▪ Identify the purpose of ESXi and vCenter Server

  ▪ Differentiate VMware migration technologies

  ▪ Differentiate VMware availability technologies

  ▪ Explain the concepts of cluster and resource pools

  ▪ Identify and explain common VMware data center products

This chapter starts with a discussion of virtual machines and what you can do with them. You will learn the purpose of the ESXi hypervisor, then bring vCenter Server into the mix, and see how it manages the vSphere environment. Then, the chapter breaks down the migration technologies with VMware and covers how to differentiate between them. Next, it provides the same breakdown with availability technologies. You will take a look at clusters and resource pools and the roles they play in a virtualized environment. Finally, you will learn about specific VMware data center products and their advantages.

Virtual Machines

This section enables you to take a deep dive into what a virtual machine is and what it does and makes it easy for you to identify a virtual machine on the test.

What Is a Virtual Machine, Anyway?

A great effort was made to make a virtual machine exactly like a physical one. In fact, a typical user should not be able to see a difference between a virtual server and a physical server. There are differences, though, and that can be a good thing.

We've already talked about physical servers in a data center and how each server is basically a bunch of components. And we've talked about the virtualization of these hardware devices in order to support virtualization. Remember, virtualization is the conversion of hardware devices into software resources. In this way, a virtual machine is an exact copy of a physical machine.

For example, a physical server could have a network interface card installed. In the same way, a virtual server has a virtual network interface card that can be installed. You can add a network interface card to a physical server, and after installing the driver, it would show up in the operating system. The same is true with a virtual machine, but the installation requires just a click of a mouse. This is because physical hardware devices were converted to software resources, which in turn allows this functionality.

Just like a physical server, each virtual machine has applications installed on an operating system running on dedicated hardware. The hardware, in this case, just happens to be virtual hardware, so although the hardware is dedicated to the virtual operating system, the underlying physical hardware can still be shared.

Remember, virtual machines do not require the physical space that physical servers do, and that translates to less power used, less cooling needed, less money spent on servers (capital expenditures), and lower management costs.

Since virtual hardware acts the same as physical hardware, no change to the operating system is required to support virtualization. The virtual hardware is as stable and dependable as physical hardware. And the operating system is installed on a virtual machine much the same way it is installed on a physical machine. Installing an operating system on a virtual machine can be done with a CD-ROM or an ISO image. The operating system enumerates the hardware and installs drivers for the hardware the same way, whether the machine is physical or virtual. Through the vSphere web client, you can connect to the console of a virtual machine to install the operating system and applications and make modifications to the virtual machine configuration.

What Can You Do with Virtual Machines?

Once your servers are virtualized, you gain a lot of flexibility. This section presents the advantages of using virtual machines and points out specific things you can do with them.

Copy and Clone   To take virtualization to the next level, you can leverage cloning. Cloning allows you to create an exact copy of a virtual machine. This is useful when you want to create a new virtual machine with the same installed applications and operating system configurations. A virtual machine is basically a small group of files. For example, the C: drive on Windows Server 2012 is represented by a single file on a datastore. Similarly, the hardware configuration is represented by a file that you can copy. This makes it easy to copy virtual machines. In the vCenter Server world, this is most easily done by cloning. This is a big deal—if you need to make a copy of a configured server, you can just clone it and have an exact copy. Imagine what it would take to make a copy of a configured physical server. You would have to deploy new hardware, install the operating system, and more.

Move Virtual Machines with vMotion   Moving a virtual machine with vMotion is one amazing capability virtualization gives us. You can move a virtual machine from one physical server to another. Imagine you have a four-host vSphere cluster on old HP hardware. The hardware falls out of support, and you need to perform some upgrades. You can buy new hardware, add the new hardware to a cluster, and just use vMotion to move the virtual machines to the new configured hosts.

VMware Distributed Resource Scheduler (DRS) uses vMotion to balance the cluster. If vMotion is not configured and working, DRS will not function. Verify that everything works in a new environment by using a test virtual machine before relying on it for production.

Take Snapshots   You can take a snapshot of a virtual machine in order to provide a mechanism to fall back to a previous configuration. You can gain a lot of confidence when you leverage snapshots in a vSphere environment.

For example, let's say you have a Windows server and are tasked with installing hot fixes. If you install a hot fix and break an installed application, you might have to restore to recover from the hot-fix installation attempt. But if you leverage snapshots, you can capture the state of the server before the installation. A snapshot can include not just the state of files on a hard drive, but CPU and memory as well. And if the installation breaks something, you can just revert to the snapshot, and it will be like you never attempted to install the hot fix. This is one way management costs are reduced by vSphere—it saves you time.

Back Up via vSphere Data Protection   Backing up is an important task that needs to be done whether the server is physical or virtual. However, backing up virtual machines provides some advantages over backing up a physical server. *When you back up a virtual machine, you are also backing up the hardware.* This is a big deal; since the physical hardware is abstracted from the hardware in the virtual machine, you can restore a virtual machine onto different hardware. vSphere Data Protection creates image-based backups. This is equivalent to bare-metal backups on physical servers. However, it is easier to create an image-based backup of a virtual machine. With vSphere Data Protection, the image-based backups of virtual machines can be used just like file-level physical machine backups. So you still have the flexibility to restore an individual file, just as you can with a physical file-level backup or physical bare-metal type of backup.

Grant Permissions   Permissions allow a lot of granularity in all aspects of security on a virtual machine, including the virtual hardware. For example, you can grant permission for a user to power on or shut down a virtual machine. For Active Directory (AD) environments, you can extend AD rights to the hardware of a virtual machine.

Deploy with Templates   Imagine that you want to create a new virtual machine complete with operating system configured and ready to go, with just a few mouse clicks. This is usually done with templates. You can convert a virtual machine into a template, and you can convert a template into a virtual machine.

Say you are tasked with rolling out 200 new web servers to handle a new web application and you have one web server configured exactly the way you want it. You can convert the virtual machine to a template and deploy 200 virtual machines from your perfect copy. This represents an incredible savings of time, and therefore, money.

Add Hardware   When running an operating system that supports "hot add," you can add a CPU to a virtual machine while the virtual machine is running. The same is true for memory, hard drives, and network cards.

There are major differences between physical and virtual machines. For example, if you are installing an additional hard drive on a physical server, you would need to power down the server and open it up before installing the hard drive. But in a virtual machine, you can add a new hard drive without powering down the server. In the same way, you can add memory, a CPU, or other devices on the fly, and without a reboot—assuming the underlying operating system supports this capability, of course. Can you imagine adding memory to a physical server while it's powered on?

WARNING *Hot add* refers to adding a CPU, memory, or hard drive space to a virtual machine while the virtual machine is running. Very impressive, but not all operating systems will allow you to do this. The more recent an operating system is, the more likely hot add will work.

ESXi Hypervisor

Let's get a little more in-depth on the ESXi hypervisor. It is important to understand the function of ESXi and the part it plays in the vSphere world. In this section, you'll take a look at the types of hypervisors and some of the roles and functions of ESXi.

There are two types of hypervisors: *hosted hypervisors* and *bare-metal hypervisors*. An example of a hosted hypervisor is VMware Workstation. A hosted hypervisor depends on the operating system to communicate to the physical hardware. You might use this type if you need to share unique hardware with the virtual machine.

Bare-metal hypervisors are installed on physical hardware. Most virtual data centers are using bare-metal hypervisors. They do not depend on any other operating system and handle any requests for physical hardware that virtual machines make. You dictate exactly how many resources a virtual machine can have. Effectively, this means you can share physical hardware devices with multiple virtual machines. ESXi is a bare-metal hypervisor.

The primary role that ESXi plays is that of traffic cop, or arbitrator, between virtual machines and physical devices. ESXi plays a part in other VMware technologies as well. For example, high availability (HA) requires that each ESXi host communicates with the other hosts so that the cluster can detect a host failure. This communication is handled by an agent that runs on the ESXi host.

ESX Product Name

ESX stands for *Elastic Sky X*. VMware's older GSX software stands for *Ground Storm X*. In both cases, the *X* does not really stand for anything. This is not on the test—we mention it just in case you are curious. And it's probably good for a trivia question. ESX is the predecessor to ESXi.

---

vCenter Server

vCenter Server is some amazing technology. It offers centralized management and advanced vSphere functionality on ESXi hosts and virtual machines in a data center. vCenter Server can be a virtual appliance deployed on a host or installed on a server running Windows.

This section discusses some of the features of vCenter Server in the virtual data center and lists specific challenges that vCenter Server addresses.

 vCenter Server is an important part of any large virtualized data center. However, vCenter Server is not required to create virtual machines. Only ESXi, the hypervisor, is required to virtualize physical servers.

When you have only one ESXi host, it's easy to manage it directly. But when the environment gets bigger and you have multiple ESXi hosts, management can get much more difficult. VMware's solution is vCenter Server. Now you can go to one place and manage all of your ESXi hosts. And now you can take advantage of advanced features provided by vCenter Server.

VMware vCenter Server provides a web interface to manage your hosts, or you can use the vSphere client. However, some features are available only in the web client. You can use vCenter Server with large and small data centers. You can manage one host and scale to a thousand hosts with one instance of vCenter Server. You can have multiple vCenter Server instances to scale even further. vCenter Server components include the identity management server, database server, application server, and web server.

The following are the most notable features provided by vCenter Server; in the following sections we'll go over the challenges each feature addresses.

- vMotion
- Distributed Resource Scheduler (DRS)
- Distributed Power Management (DPM)
- Storage vMotion
- Storage DRS
- vSphere Data Protection (VDP)
- High availability (HA)
- Fault tolerance (FT)
- vSphere Replication

vMotion

Imagine you are supporting an application that has to be running constantly. The application has been running for several years. However, the hardware is no longer supported, and you need to move the application to new hardware. This is a big problem—not to mention what would happen if the hardware fails, which would be an even bigger problem. vMotion can help you with this.

When you set up a cluster with a bunch of ESXi hypervisors, it can be a challenge to run virtual machines together that complement each other. For example, one virtual machine could be a CPU hog, while another could be a network hog, and both could be on the same

ESXi host without causing contention issues. But how do you constantly scan your virtual machines to see which would be good matches for each other? This can be done manually but can take all of your time. This is where vMotion can step in to help.

vMotion allows you to migrate a running virtual machine from one ESXi host to another ESXi host without downtime. Of course, both ESXi hosts must be using shared storage and have identical network resources configured. Since virtual machines basically exist as chunks of memory on an ESXi host, a successful migration with vMotion consists of copying this chunk of memory to another host. Because of the way vCenter Server communicates with the ESXi host, you may not notice even one network packet being dropped.

Challenges Addressed

- The need to do repairs and upgrades on hosts without shutting down running virtual machines
- Even distribution of virtual machines across ESXi hosts (DRS)

Distributed Resource Scheduler

As virtual machines use resources on the ESXi hosts, ESXi resource usage may be uneven across the cluster. The Distributed Resource Scheduler provides load balancing across the VMware cluster. This allows you to evenly distribute virtual machine load across physical hosts. DRS captures performance metrics of running virtual machines in order to make informed decisions of where to place virtual machines that need to be powered on. DRS can be set for different levels of automation. You can configure DRS to be completely automatic or to make suggestions and let you manually deploy the suggestions. DRS can also be used to isolate virtual machines from one another so that two virtual machines will not be on the same host. Alternatively, you can use DRS to keep two virtual machines on the same host.

Challenges Addressed

- The need to use hardware resources evenly across a cluster
- Deciding what host to put a virtual machine on as it is powered on
- Whether to keep virtual machines grouped or isolated

Distributed Power Management

Distributed Power Management is an interesting feature that vCenter Server provides. With DPM, you can control which hosts are available for a cluster. For example, if you have dozens of virtual machines that have high usage during the day but not at night, you can have DPM migrate virtual machines (using vMotion) to only a few hosts and power down the freed-up hosts in order to save on power and cooling costs. DPM will then power on the ESXi hosts and migrate virtual machines across all hosts before virtual machine usage goes up the next business day.

Challenge Addressed

- The need to save money on power and cooling costs

Storage vMotion

Storage vMotion is a way to migrate the storage used by a virtual machine while the virtual machine is running. You may have shared storage connected to several ESXi hosts and need to repair or upgrade the shared or backend storage array. With Storage vMotion, you can relocate the virtual machine to a different shared or backend storage array and then upgrade the freed-up storage volumes with no downtime.

Storage vMotion can also be leveraged when shared storage is not used. For example, say you have a virtual machine running on an ESXi host and the local storage on the host is used to store the virtual machine files. You can still use Storage vMotion to move this virtual machine to another host. The other host can have local or shared storage, and Storage vMotion is still an option.

Challenges Addressed

- The need to upgrade the shared or backend storage arrays that a virtual machine resides on
- The need to free up local storage on an ESXi host before any needed software or hardware repairs or upgrades are done on the ESXi host

Storage DRS

You know that vCenter Server tracks virtual machine resource usage in order to intelligently move virtual machines to ESXi hosts to load balance the cluster; Storage DRS does the same thing but for the backend storage. Disk I/O is monitored on shared storage devices in order to get the information Storage DRS needs to do its job.

Like cluster-level DRS, Storage DRS can be configured to be completely automatic. In this case, Storage DRS will automatically move virtual machines, using Storage vMotion, to level out the datastore usage on the storage array. You can also configure Storage DRS to give you suggestions on the best way to configure the virtual machine's storage and let you manually implement the suggestions.

And, like cluster-level DRS, Storage DRS can also be used to isolate virtual machines from one another, but for the storage backend. For example, if you have a database server that has high-storage I/O usage and an Exchange server that also has high-storage I/O usage, Storage DRS can be used to keep these two virtual machines separate and on different datastores.

Challenges Addressed

- Even distribution of the storage load of virtual machines across a storage array
- Isolation of virtual machines with heavy storage demands so that one busy datastore does not impact other virtual machines on the same storage array

vSphere Data Protection

Whether a server is physical or virtual, you want to protect the data on it by performing backups. Even though a virtual machine can be more resilient than physical machines, things can go wrong, and it is always a good idea to have backups.

vSphere Data Protection uses snapshots in the backup process, and the data from backups is de-duped, providing smaller sizes. vSphere Data Protection uses image-based backups, which are the same as bare-metal backups in the physical world. This allows a virtual machine restore to be a simple exercise of restoring and powering on.

vSphere Data Protection is used to back up virtual machines residing on ESXi hosts. Leveraging vCenter Server for protecting virtual machines makes backups easier and more manageable. vSphere Data Protection makes restoring a virtual machine easy, and the same backup can be used to restore a single file.

In case you have to support a different backup solution, VMware published an open set of APIs for vSphere Data Protection, called VADP, that other backup vendors can leverage in their products.

Challenges Addressed

- The need to back up virtual machines as a preventative measure against accidents and other issues
- The need for a mechanism to restore a file or set of files

High-Availability Configuration

High availability (HA) is easily recognized as one of the most important features of vCenter Server. HA protects against catastrophic hardware failures, problems with an individual virtual machine, and problems with a specific application residing on a virtual machine.

Hardware failures happen to ESXi hosts just as they do to other physical servers. High availability provides an automated way to recover from catastrophic failures. Since one ESXi host can support many virtual machines, offering a high-availability option is important. When an ESXi host goes down, the virtual machines on that host experience a sudden loss of power, not a graceful shutdown. However, the virtual machines are brought back up quickly on other ESXi hosts.

An HA-enabled cluster consists of a number of physical ESXi hosts that communicate with each other. When an ESXi host suffers a failure, other hosts in the same cluster realize there was a failure and automatically start the virtual machines back up on other ESXi hosts that are still running. vCenter Server is necessary for HA because the initial configuration is done through vCenter Server. However, once the configuration is set, vCenter Server is not needed for HA to function.

Each virtual machine in an HA cluster constantly talks to the physical host it resides on. In this way, HA can protect individual virtual machines and take action when there is a problem; HA also can automatically restart the virtual machine.

HA also provides application-level monitoring and protection. A virtual machine can be up and appear to be running normally, but an installed application can be nonresponsive. HA protection at the application level can help guard against this type of problem.

Challenges Addressed

- The need to have protection again catastrophic hardware failures
- The need to monitor virtual machines for issues
- The need to monitor an application for problems

Fault Tolerance

Sometimes you need a virtual machine up and running, no matter what. In this case, fault tolerance (FT) is a must-have feature. When you use fault tolerance, a virtual machine is mirrored to an identical virtual machine on another ESXi host. Everything that happens to one happens on the other so that everything is synced. When an ESXi host has a hardware failure, the mirror virtual machine is still up and running on the other ESXi host.

Fault tolerance is a transparent active-passive type of clustering. For these types of clusters, there is a primary virtual machine and a secondary virtual machine. There are limits to the virtual machine that is protected by fault tolerance. To enable fault tolerance on a virtual machine, it must not have more than one virtual CPU and must not have any snapshots. The virtual machine must be in an HA-enabled cluster. There are other limits as well.

Challenge Addressed

- The need to support virtual machines that cannot have any downtime

vSphere Replication

As we all know, backups are a big deal. Backups are all about protection. vSphere Replication takes this one step further and allows you to make a copy of virtual machines in your environment and put that copy in a remote location. You should store at least one copy of your backups in an offsite location. It is even better when you not only have a copy of your data, but you can also power on the copies in case of a disaster.

A large company might want to leverage vSphere Replication to centralize data. Virtual machines in branch offices can be synced over to the main data center to protect the branch office data as well as to provide a way to recover if the branch office has a disaster. Using vSphere Replication, you can also restore to a certain point in time. Setup is easy, as is monitoring the replication.

When configuring replication, you have the opportunity to choose historical point-in-time retention. This means you can revert a virtual machine to any earlier replicas. For example, after you back up your virtual machines every day for the last month, you can restore a virtual machine to any point-in-time replica for the last month.

Challenges Addressed

- Protect against disaster affecting the entire data center
- Centralize data in a large organization
- Multiple point-in-time restore

Migration

This section presents various types of migrations and the ways you can use them in your environment.

Migrations are one of the great features of VMware solutions. Being able to move a running virtual machine to another host is impressive. There are other types of migrations as well. Here is a short list; we'll discuss each one:

- vMotion
- Cold
- Storage vMotion
- Suspended VM
- Physical to virtual (P2V)
- Virtual to virtual (V2V)

vMotion migration is typically the first type of migration people are exposed to. Coming from the world of physical-only servers, it is kind of exciting. vMotion migration is sometimes referred to as a *hot* migration because the virtual machine is running. vMotion moves a running virtual machine to a different ESXi host in the same cluster. This type of move requires vCenter Server to manage the cluster as well as a network port to be configured for vMotion.

Cold migrations are almost like vMotion migrations, except that the virtual machine is not running; it is powered down. Cold migrations are more flexible than using regular vMotion. Cold migrations can be used to move a virtual machine between data centers, as long as both data centers are on the same vCenter Server instance. Cold migrations can move the virtual machine to a different datastore. And a cold migration is more likely to succeed than a hot migration.

Like a cold migration, a *Storage vMotion* migration relocates virtual machine storage to a different datastore. This is handy when you need to upgrade a storage subsystem and you do not want to impact any running virtual machines. You can also combine vMotion and the Storage vMotion at the same time. Combining these will let you move the virtual machine's files and change the host at the same time.

A *suspended VM* migration is a lot like a regular vMotion migration. Suspended and regular vMotion migrations are considered *hot* because in both cases the virtual machine is running. The primary reason to suspend a virtual machine on an ESXi host is for troubleshooting. (You should not see any questions on the exam on this topic; it is included here for completeness.)

P2V migrations convert a physical computer to a virtual one. This makes migrating to VMware easy. For example, say you have a web server running on physical hardware. You can run VMware vCenter Converter, target the web server, and have a copy of the physical server created on an ESXi host.

V2V migrations are exactly like P2V migrations except that the source machine is already a virtual machine. At first glance, this might not look very useful. However, being able to migrate a virtual machine to another virtual machine does bring some flexibility. For example, migrating from Hyper-V and VMware Workstation to ESXi would be considered a V2V migration.

A big part of managing virtual machines with vSphere is migrating them to free up an ESXi host before rebooting or upgrading the host hardware. Or you might want to migrate virtual machines off backend storage so you can update the storage hardware—that kind of thing. Migrations add to the flexibility of virtualization. Once you get used to this process, you will not be able to live without it.

The first time you migrate a virtual machine, you can appreciate how cool it is. Installed applications no longer have to be tied to a physical server. The first time I moved a virtual machine to a new host, it was kind of amazing. Now I can reboot a host without affecting virtual machines, and I can move the virtual machine to any other host in the cluster.

High Availability

This section covers the availability features of VMware and what this availability can do for you in your environment. We'll also discuss the types of availability.

In a general sense, availability in VMware extends to more than just ESXi hosts. VMware high availability (HA) is the foundation for availability in VMware. VMware HA is enabled on the cluster level. You can add HA to an existing cluster or create a new cluster and enable HA before adding hosts to the cluster. Once a cluster is HA enabled, this

VMware solution can detect not only host failures but also virtual machine failures and even application failures, and then it can take corrective action.

By leveraging VMware HA, companies can minimize the downtime resulting from a host failure. Before virtualization, a physical server would have an issue and send the support team into overdrive resolving the problem. Sometimes, finding a solution to the problem can be time-consuming. With VMware HA, a physical host can experience a failure and the virtual machines will be restarted on other, still running, hosts, thereby minimizing the downtime experienced. This is especially important when companies suffer monetary loss because of outages.

Let's discuss HA in a little more depth. We can break down availability into four basic groups:

- Host HA
- Virtual machine HA
- Applications HA
- Fault tolerance (FT)

Host HA

Host HA is the basic VMware HA that is most often enabled on VMware clusters. It is a simple matter to enable HA through edit settings (Home➤Inventory➤Hosts and Clusters➤select cluster➤Edit settings) Figure 3.1 shows what the setting looks like in the vSphere client.

FIGURE 3.1   Enabling HA

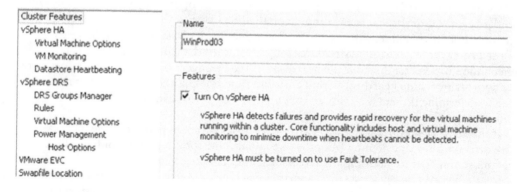

VMware HA hosts now have a simple master-slave relationship. Only one host in a cluster is the master. Don't worry; you don't have to select a host as an administrator to be the master node. This happens through an election process that is initiated every time a cluster is enabled or reconfigured, among other things. The ESXi server with access to the most datastores wins. If there is a tie, the lexically highest managed object ID (MOID) wins.

VMware HA has no dependency on DNS resolution. In the past, if DNS resolution was not 100 percent, there could be major issues. Fortunately, this is no longer the case. In fact, VMware HA has no external dependencies.

To improve reliability, VMware HA now communicates through the shared storage as well as the management network to detect a host failure. This is a big improvement and was put in place to reduce false positives of a host failure. Communicating over shared storage introduced *datastore heartbeating* to VMware HA. All the hosts are connected through the shared storage, and datastore heartbeating works by each host in a VMware cluster locking a file on shared storage. However, this generally is used only after a management network heartbeat failure.

Virtual Machine HA

Virtual machine monitoring is enabled on the cluster level. If you have virtual machines that you want to enable virtual machine monitoring on, the cluster must be configured for HA first. By default, virtual machine HA is not enabled.

Before you can enable virtual machine monitoring, the cluster must already be enabled for HA. You cannot enable virtual machine monitoring during cluster creation. You must enable HA on the cluster and configure virtual machine monitoring afterward.

Another requirement for virtual machine monitoring is that VMware Tools must be installed. The method VMware uses to monitor individual virtual machines starts with the VMware Tools heartbeat. During normal virtual machine operation, VMware Tools will send a heartbeat to the HA agent running on the ESXi host.

Sometimes a virtual machine will be so busy that it can't bother to send the heartbeat to the HA agent. That is, if a virtual machine is using all the CPU resources, it is not uncommon to miss sending out the heartbeat. If the HA agent on the ESXi host does not get a virtual machine heartbeat within a certain time frame, the HA agent takes the next step to determine if there is a failure. That certain time frame can vary and is called the *failure interval*.

If the ESXi agent does not get a heartbeat over the failure interval, the agent checks for disk or network traffic coming from the virtual machine for 2 minutes (configurable as a custom setting) before marking the virtual machine as failed, requiring that it be reset. To prevent repeated attempts restarting a virtual machine, VMware keeps track of the number of resets within a given time, known as the *reset period*. After vSphere HA restarts a virtual machine three times, it makes no attempt to restart a virtual machine until the reset period has elapsed.

The settings for virtual machine HA are configurable. You can choose a sensitivity level of high, medium, low, or a custom setting. A high setting means a 30-second failure interval, with a reset period of 1 hour. This means the HA agent would wait until 30 seconds pass without a VMware Tools heartbeat, and then check for disk and network traffic for 2 minutes before marking the virtual machine as needing a restart. The ESXi agent will allow only three restarts during the reset period. Three is the default number. However, the number can be customized with the maximum per VM resets setting. If the virtual machine has been restarted three times within the last hour, virtual machine HA would not restart the virtual machine again during the 1-hour reset period.

Be careful when setting the sensitivity level on virtual machines. You may want to start with a low setting and gradually modify the setting to determine how well the virtual machines handle monitoring. Also important to note is that deleting snapshots does not count toward disk I/O for the virtual machine; if monitoring is checking disk I/O to determine whether the virtual machine should be reset based on the sensitivity configuration, and the virtual machine is committing snapshots, the disk I/O from the deletion of the snapshots is not picked up as I/O that would allow the virtual machine to be marked as needing a reset.

Note that if a virtual machine is restarted by HA, the VMware software will take a screenshot of the console of the virtual machine, which is stored with the working files of the virtual machine. This is used as a troubleshooting tool to help you discover what went wrong with the virtual machine.

Application HA

Application-level HA requires use of a software development kit (SDK) developed just for this purpose or applications that already work with application HA. Many companies create in-house applications and leverage application monitoring through this SDK. You also have to set up customized heartbeats for the application. Application monitoring behaves like virtual machine monitoring, restarting the virtual machine when necessary.

Fault Tolerance

Fault tolerance is an interesting feature and serves a specific purpose. Fault tolerance was developed to provide the ultimate virtual availability solution—just like HA on steroids, designed to provide continuous availability.

In normal VMware HA, the virtual machines hosted on a failed ESXi server will be restarted on alternate hosts. But what if you cannot handle the restart? What if you are running an application that is so important, you cannot afford any downtime? Used to be, you would use OS-level clustering to achieve no downtime. However, OS-level clustering can be complex and prone to issues. Now you can leverage fault tolerance.

When you enable fault tolerance on a virtual machine, an identical virtual machine is created on another host. Only one of the virtual machines is the master, and it does all the writes. There is a heartbeat between the two virtual machines, and each is a mirror of the other. The VMware technology for this is called VMware vLockstep. It keeps not only the two disks the same, but also the memory state. If a failure is detected, the mirror takes over as if nothing happened.

Both virtual machines have the same IP and MAC address and appear as one virtual machine in the vSphere client or web client.

 WARNING   When you enable fault tolerance on a virtual machine, it shows only one object in the client. However, resources for two virtual machines are used. You may have to adjust your design to compensate for fault tolerance if you plan to use it.

There are some requirements to use fault tolerance. You need a dedicated network connection of at least 1 GB. If you have multiple virtual machines leveraging fault tolerance on a host, you should consider a 10 GB network connection just for fault tolerance.

Clusters and Resource Pools

This section describes the advantages of clusters and resource pools, as well as the challenges that clusters and resources pools address.

Clusters

A *cluster* is a set of physical hosts logically grouped so that you can manage the aggregate CPU and memory resources of the hosts as one collection. In the VMware sense, a cluster is primarily used to gain availability and load balancing of virtual machines. Figure 3.2 shows what a cluster looks like in the client.

FIGURE 3.2   Cluster icons

When you select a cluster in the vSphere client, the Summary tab gives you the total CPU resources, total memory, and total storage. You should think of a VMware cluster as the total resources available for virtual machines. When you power on a virtual machine, it can be put on any ESXi host in the cluster (assuming no affinity rules).

This is an example of the abstraction of virtual machines from the underlying physical hardware.

Using clusters is one way to scale your data center to manageable chunks. A cluster can have up to 32 hosts and 4,000 virtual machines. And a cluster is an HA, DRS, and DPM boundary—meaning HA, DRS, and DPM cannot cross clusters.

Resource Pools

Resource pools provide a way to allocate the aggregate computing power and other resources of the cluster. Resource pools can be hierarchical and nested. There is a maximum of 1,600 resource pools per cluster. Although you can assign a resource pool to an individual ESXi host, you can also assign a resource pool to a cluster. You can create a new resource pool only if you have a data center defined with at least one host.

Let's start with an example of a company named NewPaper that specializes in providing recycled paper to industries concerned about their environmental impact. This small company uses two ESXi hosts in a cluster to provide resources. Each host has two CPUs with eight cores, each running at 2.7 GHz and 132 GB of memory. This is a rather typical configuration. The cluster summary could look something like Figure 3.3.

FIGURE 3.3   Cluster summary example

General		Resources		
Manufacturer:	HP	CPU usage: **2739 MHz**		Capacity
Model:	ProLiant BL460c Gen8			16 x 2.699 GHz
CPU Cores:	16 CPUs x 2.699 GHz	Memory usage: **24526.00 MB**		Capacity
Processor Type:	Intel(R) Xeon(R) CPU ES-2680 0 @ 2.70GHz			131037.20 MB
License:	VMware vSphere 5 Enterprise - Licensed for 2 physical CP...	Storage	Status	Drive Type
Processor Sockets:	2	DMZII101-3PAR	Normal	Non-SSD
Cores per Socket:	8	DMZII102-3PAR	Normal	Non-SSD
Logical Processors:	32	DMZII103-3PAR	Normal	Non-SSD
Hyperthreading:	Active	DMZII104-3PAR	Normal	Non-SSD
Number of NICs:	4	esxdmz04_das	Normal	Non-SSD
State:	Connected			

The NewPaper finance department has 10 critical virtual machines, and you would like to allocate 16 GB of memory and 4 GHz of CPU for each one. These are critical servers and must be kept running. So the entire resource pool would get 160 GB of memory and 40 GHz of processing power.

To create the resource pool, just right-click the cluster and select New Resource Pool. A dialog box comes up and gives you a prompt to name the resource pool and allocate the resources appropriately (see Figure 3.4).

FIGURE 3.4   Creating the resource pool

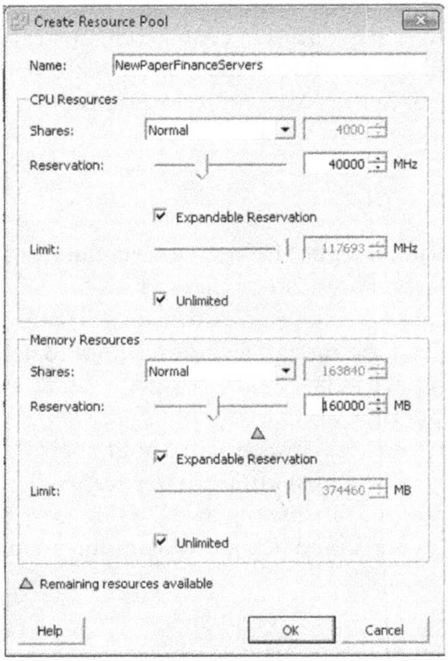

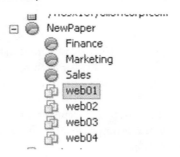

Click OK, and the resource pool will be created with the required reservation. The icon for the new resource pool is shaped like a pie (see Figure 3.5).

FIGURE 3.5   Resource Pool icon

Because resource pools are so handy, other NewPaper departments become jealous and demand their own resource pools. Thankfully, you can have nested resource pools. After a little renaming, the NewPaper structure could look Figure 3.6.

FIGURE 3.6   Nested resource pools

Now you can micromanage all the resource pools to whatever makes sense. You can also assign rights to resource pools. Things can get a little tricky at this point, with multiple resource pools and nested pools. The exam expects you to know what resource pools are, but not much more than that.

Real World Scenario

Resource Pools

You have to be careful and think things through when setting up resource pools. I have seen three resource pools created off the root cluster with varying shares so that one was for important virtual machines, one was for medium, and one was for low. This worked well until the number of virtual machines in the important virtual machine resource pool had many virtual machines. At some point, performance problems creep up. In this case, so many virtual machines were in the important resource pool that the few servers in the low pools did much better and actually ended up with more shares per virtual machine. Simple math in hindsight: the number of shares configured on the resource pools is divided by the number of virtual machines in the resource pools. If you have 100 virtual machines in one resource pools and 3 virtual machines in another resource pools, the 3 virtual machines will get more resources than 1 of the virtual machines in the 100 virtual machine resource pools. So always monitor all aspects of your VMware installation over time.

Other VMware Data Center Products

This section describes some of VMware's commonly used products for data center virtualization:

- vRealize Operations (previously called vCenter Operations Manager)
- vSphere Data Protection
- NSX (VMware's network virtualization product)
- Virtual SAN
- vCenter Site Recovery Manager

vCenter Operations Manager

vCenter Operations Manager is one of those "tie everything together" products. After you have a virtualized data center, you have to be able to look in and see how things are going, and what you can do in order to make things better. vCenter Operations Manager works with VMware ESXi, as well as Amazon, Hyper-V, and physical servers. It provides the ability to see problems coming in order to shorten resolution time. And you can get consistent configuration with policy-based automation.

vSphere Data Protection

vSphere Data Protection is an attempt to back up your virtualized data center the correct way. This product was written with virtual machines in mind and to leverage the flexibility that virtual machines provide. All the basics are covered: backup, restore, and restore a file from a backup while minimizing storage space and network bandwidth. There is a version that comes with Essentials Plus licensing and an advanced version that provides more-advanced functionality.

 If a question on the exam talks about backing up or restoring a virtual machine, there is a chance it is referring to vSphere Data Protection. Just remember, protection equals backing up and restoring.

NSX

NSX is one of the advanced products that you might not hear about unless you are looking at the in-depth technology that VMware provides. NSX is all about networking in the virtualized world. It does a good job of deploying firewall-type functionality to all the virtual machines. When you start reading about NSX, you will most likely find it very impressive. For this test, you should know what NSX is but should not have to go down the rabbit hole too far (though, feel free to do so if you find it interesting).

Virtual SAN

VMware's Virtual SAN provides a pseudo storage area network (SAN) for ESXi hosts. You need at least three ESXi hosts in a cluster to leverage Virtual SAN. You enable Virtual SAN by browsing to a cluster in the vSphere web client, editing the settings, and enabling Virtual SAN.

VMware Virtual SAN requires fast local storage. Each host must have solid-state drives (SSDs), along with spinning disks. There are other requirements as well, and VMware provides good documentation on the subject.

You can have an ESXi cluster with only local host storage; the local storage is treated like shared storage, such as a SAN backend. You can still move virtual machines with vMotion and even use Storage vMotion to move backend storage used by virtual machines. Virtual SAN is similar to Microsoft Exchange Database Availability Groups (DAGs) to host mailbox databases on multiple servers. This is a real boon for home labs and small businesses that cannot afford a typical SAN backend solution.

vCenter Site Recovery Manager

Backups are mandatory. If you don't use backups, you are risking all the data you have on your computer system. vCenter Site Recovery Manager is the step after backups. Basically, vCenter Site Recovery Manager provides a way to bring all of your virtual machines up in another data center. When you step back and think about how complicated this can get, you will realize it is pretty amazing.

vCenter Site Recovery Manager is used to not only bring up your data center in another location after a site disaster, but also to test your disaster-recovery process. It is easy to sense exam questions that may have something to do with vCenter Site Recovery Manager when you see *replication* or *failure of an entire data center.*

vCenter Site Recovery Manager coordinates the process, and you have a couple of options for replication of the virtual machines: storage array–based replication and vSphere Replication. Storage array–based replication is more of the old-school way of replicating data between two sites. vSphere Replication is a proprietary replication engine designed to reduce bandwidth needs considerably. After the initial seed, vSphere Replication works hard to replicate only changes. vSphere Replication can even replicate a running virtual machine.

Summary

This chapter talked about what virtual machines are and what you can do with them. Virtual machines are basically digital clones of physical servers, and you can copy them, move them, back them up, take snapshots, and deploy them.

We talked about the bare-metal ESXi hypervisor and the hosted VMware Workstation product and their differences. We also covered the primary role of the VMware ESXi hypervisor: resource traffic cop.

We went a little more in depth on vCenter Server and how it is used to manage your environment. A lot of virtual machine management starts with a VMware vCenter Server, so it is essential for many tasks. We talked about the features and challenges addressed by VMware vCenter Server, vMotion, DRS, DPM, Storage vMotion, Storage DRS, HA, and FT.

We touched on availability and broke it down into the four types: host HA, virtual machine HA, applications HA, and FT. Host HA is the first type of high availability that most companies leverage with VMware. If a question on the exam talks about HA generically, assume HA for hosts.

We went over clusters and resource pools, what they are, and what you can do with them. We also covered how clusters and resource pools enable you to manage the aggregate resources of the hosts in a cluster so that you manage the total CPU and memory resources. We mentioned how you can use resource pools to further manage groups of virtual machines.

We also covered other VMware data center products such as vRealize Operations (previously known as vSphere Operations Manager) which is one of the best solutions for managing ongoing operations. vSphere Data Protection is VMware's solution for backing up and restoring virtual machines. NSX makes it easy to bring enterprise-level firewall technology to all of your virtual machines. Virtual SAN is a contender for a storage solution for small companies and development environments that cannot justify the cost of an expensive SAN storage backend. And, of course, Site Recovery Manager is targeted toward companies that want a grown-up disaster-recovery solution that can get your data center back up and running in a short time.

Exam Essentials

Know what a virtual machine is and its capabilities.   You need to be able to identify a virtual machine and a physical server and to know the capabilities of a virtual machine.

Know what ESXi and vCenter Server are used for.   The role of the ESXi host is called the hypervisor. The hypervisor is the resource traffic cop between virtual machines and the physical host hardware. vCenter Server manages many of the advanced technologies.

Know the types of migrations.   You can perform six types of migrations with virtual machines in VMware:

vMotion   Moves a VM from one host to another.

Storage vMotion   Moves VM files to a different datastore.

Cold migration   Moves VMs while powered off.

Suspended VM   Is like vMotion migration, with VM suspended.

P2V   Is migration from physical to virtual.

V2V   Is migration from virtual to virtual.

Differentiate between availability technologies.   The core vSphere components include several types of availability technologies. The core stuff does not include vCenter Site Recovery Manager; however, the core stuff does cover vCenter Server and ESXi HA technologies.

Understand the concept of clusters and resource pools.   Clusters and resource pools play a major role in most virtual data center designs and should be leveraged. You need to know what a cluster is, what it is used for, and what role resource pools play.

Know what VMware products are used for different purposes.   The questions you see on a test could be for specific VMware products. It will be helpful to know, even at a high level, what challenge each product is meant to address.

Review Questions

You can find the answers in Appendix A.

1. The CTO of your company drops by and tells you he just came back from a conference where he heard horror stories about people testing their disaster recovery plans and breaking the production data center. He has no clue how anything actually works. What product do you tell him about in an attempt to calm him down?

    A. Fault tolerance (FT)

    B. High availability (HA)

    C. vSphere Data Protection

    D. vCenter Site Recovery Manager

2. One of the power supplies in one of your hosts goes out. You are worried that the server no longer has a spare power supply. What is the first thing you would try to do in order to free up the ESXi host?

    A. Power down the ESXi host

    B. Use vMotion to migratethe virtual machines to another host

    C. Use Storage vMotion to move the virtual machines on the host to another storage volume

    D. Enable vSphere replication on the virtual machines

3. The CTO of your company stops by your office and wants to understand how this "VMware stuff" works. You try to explain the basics. What one-line explanation would you use to explain the hypervisor?

    A. A virtual file system exposed to hosts in a cluster

    B. Movement of a virtual machine to a different host

    C. A layer between the physical hardware and virtual machines

    D. An agent that runs on ESXi

4. Microsoft just released an operating system patch that is rated critical. Your manager tells you that you need to install this patch right now. You download the patch and log on to the server. Just before you install the patch, what is one thing you can do to quickly roll back the server to this starting point?

    A. Use DRS to balance the cluster

    B. Isolate the virtual machine in the cluster

    C. Move the virtual machine to the virtual SAN

    D. Take a snapshot of the virtual machine

5. You work for a financial firm that invests money for clients. Because of Sarbanes-Oxley requirements, you need to monitor your VMware environment and produce an audit report for management. What VMware product can help you out here?

    A. vCenter Configuration Manager

    B. vCenter Operations Manager

    C. vSphere Data Protection

    D. vSphere Replication

6. You are in a meeting with the financial and HR departments. Each department is anxious to use VMware but also worried that the other department will use more of the resources. These two departments will share a cluster. What is the best way to split up these resources?

    A. Limit the financial department to one ESX host

    B. Limit the HR department to four virtual machines

    C. Create resource pools for the two departments

    D. Create a separate data center object for each department

7. One of your coworkers recently rolled out new patches for all of the Windows virtual machines in your environment. Your coworker is a pretty smart guy, and you would expect the correct processes were followed. One application owner complains about his server acting strange, though. Assuming you would like to remove the recent patch from the app owner's Windows server, what do you expect to be able to do?

    A. Remove the patch through add/remove programs

    B. Revert to the snapshot taken before the patch installation

    C. Reinstall the operating system and application

    D. Open a ticket with Microsoft to troubleshoot

8. The head of the financial department talks to you in a meeting set up to discuss requirements for some special application servers. He tells you these servers are directly tied to incoming revenue and cannot suffer any downtime. He expects 100 percent uptime. What VMware solution would be the best bet for him?

    A. vSphere Data Protection

    B. vCenter Site Recovery Manager

    C. vCenter Operations Manager

    D. Fault tolerance

9. You are in charge of a small company with three VMware clusters hosting about a hundred virtual machines. You leverage distributed switches for all ESXi hosts. Routing and firewall rules on your network infrastructure are getting complicated. Several server outages have been blamed on small network changes in your firewall or routers. In the near future, new planned rules promise to make things even more complicated. What VMware product makes the most sense to leverage here?

   A. vRealize Operations (vCenter Operations Manager)

   B. vCenter Server

   C. vSphere Data Protection

   D. NSX

10. You work for a small company that has only three ESXi hosts in a cluster. You do not have a backend storage solution in place. Each ESXi host has two hard disk drives and one solid-state drive. What is your best storage option for hosting virtual machines?

   A. Virtual SAN

   B. External HDD

   C. Local storage

   D. vCenter Server

11. You need to deploy two dozen new virtual machines in your ESXi cluster. What is the best method to accomplish this task?

   A. Copy individual VMDK files to new locations.

   B. Leverage templates to deploy new virtual machines.

   C. Clone existing virtual machines.

   D. Install new virtual machines from ISO files.

12. What VMware product do you need to enable virtual machine monitoring?

   A. vCenter Server

   B. vCenter Operations Manager

   C. vCenter Configuration Manager

   D. vSphere Data Protection

13. What VMware product can analyze ESXi and virtual machine statistics and provide a visual representation of the health of the environment?

   A. vCenter Server

   B. vSphere Data Protection

   C. vCenter Site Recovery Manager

   D. vCenter Operations Manager

14. You work for a small company that finally can afford a SAN solution. You put the solution in place and can finally have shared storage for your ESXi hosts. What do you use to move the existing virtual machines to the new shared storage?

  A. vMotion

  B. Storage I/O Control

  C. Manual copy

  D. Storage vMotion

15. The storage engineer in your company recently added 10 new SAN volumes to your ESXi hosts. You would like to take advantage of the new storage and spread your virtual machines across more spindles. What is the best way to get what you want?

  A. Use Storage vMotion on selected virtual machines.

  B. Leverage Storage DRS.

  C. Use Storage I/O Control to balance the virtual machines.

  D. Use vMotion to move the virtual machines.

16. What is the biggest benefit of migrating physical application servers to virtual machines hosted on ESXi?

  A. Less physical memory used

  B. Server consolidation

  C. Expanded product life cycle

  D. Centralized backup

17. You work for a large company that does a yearly disaster-recovery exercise. The company has a dedicated site for disaster recovery but spends most of the time during the exercise setting up the backup server to restore physical servers and making sure the hardware that is being restored is just like the original physical server. What VMware product makes a disaster-recovery test a much easier exercise?

  A. Storage DRS

  B. vCenter Site Recovery Manager

  C. vMotion

  D. Storage vMotion

18. You work for a company that just rolled out new SAN storage. The SAN storage is expensive. You would like to put all of your virtual machine files on shared storage but do not want to buy more right away. Your ESXi hosts have a single hard disk drive with the ESXi hypervisor installed. What can you leverage that will use the least amount of the expensive SAN storage?

  A. Thin provisioning

  B. Storage vMotion

  C. Virtual SAN

  D. SAN profiling

19. After rolling out a new SAN solution, you use Storage vMotion to move virtual machines around and balance out storage use. What could you use to do the same thing with even less effort?

   A. Storage DRS

   B. Storage vMotion

   C. vMotion

   D. vCenter SRM

20. You are talking to an application owner who created an application that load balances work between several servers by using Microsoft Network Load Balancing. The application owner asks if anything needs to be changed after virtualizing the physical application servers. What is the best answer?

   A. No changes are necessary.

   B. A new hard drive will need to be added to the virtual machine.

   C. The virtualized servers will need to be on several hosts.

   D. A new cluster will need to be added.

Chapter

4

Storage in a VMware Environment

This chapter covers how storage is used in a VMware virtual environment. You will start by comparing physical storage and virtual storage, followed by shared storage and the VMware products that require it. You will then look at the storage types that are supported by VMware, including local storage, Fibre Channel, iSCSI, and the Network File System, and explore the advantages and disadvantages of each. You will examine the Virtual Machine File System and its advantages and compare it to the Network File System.

Once you understand these storage types, you will review three types of disk provisioning: thick provision eager zeroed, thick provision lazy zeroed, and thin provision. You will look at the advantages and disadvantages of these disk provisioning types and review usage cases for thin provisioned drives. In the final section, you will review some of the VMware products that are used to manage and support the storage environment. By the end of the chapter, you will have a better understanding of storage in a VMware environment and will be able to tackle any questions about storage on the exam.

Physical vs. Virtual Storage

This section presents the concepts of physical and virtual storage so you can develop a basic understanding of what each of them are. It also introduces the idea of shared storage. You will look at the VMware products and technologies that require shared storage to operate properly.

Physical storage is the underlying physical hardware that provides storage to the virtual environment. This can include physical hard drives in the ESXi hosts or storage arrays that the ESXi hosts connect to over the network or over specialized storage area networks (SANs).

**Examples of Physical
Storage**

Standard Hard Drives   USB Drives   Drive Arrays

Virtual storage is an abstract view of the physical storage that is available to the virtual machines as it is presented by the ESXi hosts. The ESXi hosts present the storage to the virtual machines as if it were standard hard disks within the virtual machines. The underlying physical storage can be of any type that is compatible with ESXi hosts. It can even contain multiple types of storage from different vendors at the same time, and they would all appear as standard hard disks to the virtual machines. Because the storage has been virtualized (abstracted), the virtual machines are not aware of the underlying hardware and see it only as available storage. Also, because the storage is virtualized, a virtual machine can have different drives that reside on different physical hardware. This can be useful when setting up certain types of virtual servers, such as database servers that need a high-performance drive to hold rapidly changing data.

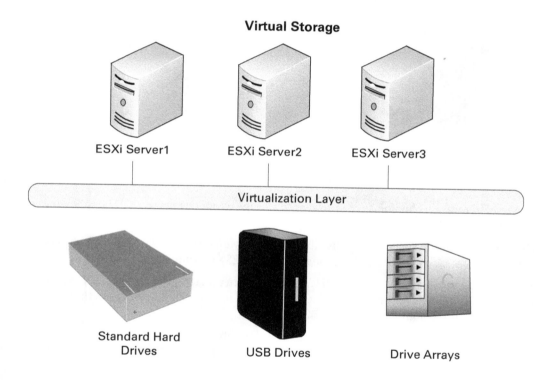

What Is Shared Storage?

Shared storage is physical storage that is available to multiple ESXi hosts at the same time. The availability of shared storage is integral to many of the features of a VMware virtual environment. Shared storage is usually contained in storage arrays that are external to the ESXi hosts, but recently released VMware technologies allow unused internal drives on ESXi hosts to be aggregated and used as shared storage.

Shared Storage

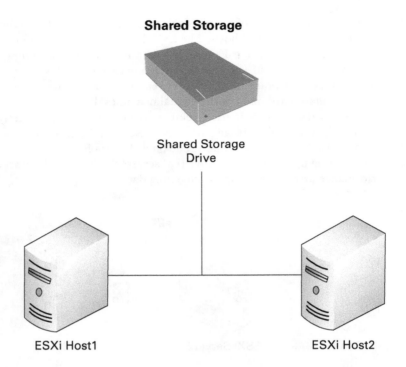

Shared Storage
Drive

ESXi Host1   ESXi Host2

Many VMware technologies require shared storage to operate correctly. The following is a list of these VMware technologies:

Distributed Power Management   Distributed Power Management (DPM) uses vMotion to migrate virtual machines off an ESXi host before the ESXi host is powered down.

High Availability   High availability (HA) restarts virtual machines on other ESXi hosts if their host has failed. The virtual machines must be located on shared storage so that they are available to the nonfailed ESXi hosts.

Storage Distributed Resource Scheduler   Storage Distributed Resource Scheduler (SDRS) migrates virtual machines from one shared datastore to another based on the storage load on each datastore.

Storage vMotion   Storage vMotion (svMotion) is used to move virtual machine files from one shared datastore to another.

The newest version of svMotion allows a virtual machine to be Storage vMotioned from any datastore to any other datastore in the data center. This would include virtual machines that are located on local ESXi host drives.

VM Storage Profiles   VM storage profiles are used to move virtual machine files from one shared datastore to another based on the performance level of the datastore.

vMotion   vMotion is used to move running virtual machines from one ESXi host to another. If either of the ESXi hosts is unable to see the datastores that contain the virtual machine, the vMotion operation will fail.

> **WARNING**   Only very small virtual environments can run effectively without shared storage. Environments without shared storage can suffer from the "all your eggs in one basket" problem. If an ESXi host with a large number of virtual machines running on its local storage fails, all of the virtual machines will be down until the ESXi host can be brought back up, if it can be brought back up at all.

Now that you have a better understanding of how VMware uses storage, let's take a look at the types of storage that are supported in a VMware environment.

VMware Storage Types

This section introduces storage technologies that are available for use in a VMware virtual environment, including the advantages and disadvantages of each of them. You will start with local storage, then look at Fibre Channel and iSCSI storage, and finally Network File System storage. At the end of this section, you will have a better understanding of the types of storage that are available and their strengths and weaknesses.

Local Storage

Local storage is essentially the drives that are physically located in the ESXi host, also referred to as *direct attached storage* (DAS). The following are advantages and disadvantages of using local storage in your virtual environment:

Advantages

- Local storage is easy to configure.
- Local storage is relatively inexpensive.
- Local storage can make the installation of ESXi hosts less complicated.

Disadvantages

- vMotion does not work for virtual machines stored on local disks.
- Local storage cannot be configured as a raw device mapping—see the "What Is a Raw Device Mapping?" sidebar for more detail.
- HA cannot be used for virtual machines stored on local storage.

Many companies will use local storage for the system disks of their ESXi hosts. They will then use some type of shared storage for the datastores that will contain their virtual machine files. This allows them the ease of installation that local storage provides and the advantages that shared storage provides for virtual machines.

What Is a Raw Device Mapping?

A *raw device mapping (RDM)* is a virtual drive pointer in VMware that points to a raw physical storage device. An RDM allows a virtual machine to have direct access to an external storage device. RDMs can be useful for machines that require direct control over a storage LUN. In the past, RDMs may have provided better performance for accessing a drive than Virtual Machine File System (VMFS), but advances in VMware technology have allowed VMFS volumes to provide the same performance as RDMs. The main use for RDMs is for certain types of clustering such as Microsoft SQL clusters, which require RDMs for their data drives.

Fibre Channel

Fibre Channel is a shared storage technology that connects the ESXi hosts to a storage array by using special cards called *host bus adapters* and fiber-optic cables and switches. The following are advantages and disadvantages of using Fibre Channel storage in your virtual environment:

Advantages of Fibre Channel Storage

- Fibre Channel provides very high performance.
- ESXi hosts using Fibre Channel storage can be configured for boot-from-SAN.

Disadvantages of Fibre Channel Storage

- Fibre Channel is difficult to configure.
- Fibre Channel can be expensive.
- Fibre Channel requires additional hardware to be added to the ESXi hosts.

Boot-from-SAN

Boot-from-SAN is a technology that allows physical servers to be built without any internal storage drives. The boot drive of the server is located on a storage area network. During the bootup sequence, the server will connect to its boot drive over the SAN and continue booting as if the boot drive was locally installed. Boot-from-SAN servers tend to experience fewer hardware issues, since the drives are located on the SAN. SAN drives are usually of very high quality and are configured in arrays that will continue functioning without interruption even if a single drive failure occurs. The issue with using boot-from-SAN is that it can be expensive to add SAN cards to a server and to purchase additional SAN storage.

iSCSI

iSCSI is an alternative to Fibre Channel storage; it connects the ESXi hosts to a storage array by using standard network cards and acts like a standard SCSI connection. iSCSI can even use the network cards that you are using to connect your ESXi host to the network, but that is not recommended. If you do use the same network cards for iSCSI and your ESXi host connection, a surge in iSCSI traffic can cause your ESXi host to become unavailable.

The following are advantages and disadvantages of using iSCSI storage in your virtual environment:

Advantages

- iSCSI is relatively easy to configure.
- iSCSI is less expensive than Fibre Channel.
- ESXi hosts using iSCSI storage can be configured for boot-from-SAN.

Disadvantages

- iSCSI provides lesser performance than Fibre Channel.
- iSCSI may require additional network cards to be added to the ESXi hosts.

 Many recent advances in iSCSI storage have greatly increased its performance. Therefore, many companies that would not have considered iSCSI storage in the past are now looking at it as a way to save money over using Fibre Channel.

Network File System

Network File System (NFS) is a shared storage technology that connects the ESXi hosts to a storage array by using standard network cards. The following are advantages and disadvantages of using Network File System storage in your virtual environment:

Advantages

- Network File System can be easy to configure.
- Network File System can be inexpensive when compared to other shared storage options.

Disadvantages

- Network File System does not support the Virtual Machine File System (discussed in depth in the next section).
- Network File System provides lesser performance than Fibre Channel or iSCSI storage performance.

Virtual Machine File System

This section covers the *Virtual Machine File System (VMFS)*. We will start by discussing what the VMFS is and then compare datastores that are using it against those that are using the Network File System (NFS). By the end of the section, you will have a better understanding of the VMFS and how it performs compared to the NFS.

The VMFS is a file system designed by VMware that allows multiple ESXi hosts to have read-write access to the file system at the same time. It is designed for high performance and to provide optimal performance for virtual machines.

The VMFS vs. the NFS

In the past, significant differences existed between the VMFS and the NFS. We could not use snapshots on virtual machines contained on NFS datastores, and we could not use vMotion on virtual machines stored on NFS datastores—though we could do both of these things with VMFS. Because of technological advances, the only remaining difference is that NFS volumes cannot be configured as RDMs. This can limit their use for some types of clustering and high-end database usage. There is also a debate about the storage performance of NFS datastores when compared to VMFS datastores. Some believe that VMFS performs more quickly, while others believe there is little to no difference.

 Most of the environments I have worked in use either Fibre Channel or iSCSI connectivity and VMFS datastores. This could be because these company networks are very large and were developed years ago when VMFS datastores had definite advantages over NFS datastores. Some modern NFS implementations can perform as well as these other solutions. NFS or iSCSI can be good solutions for home study labs because they reduce the cost and complexity of setting up shared storage.

Disk Provisioning

This section presents an overview of VMware disk provisioning, including the types of provisioning allowed by VMware and the advantages and disadvantages of each. By the end of this section, you should have a good understanding of what disk provisioning is and be able to determine which type you should use in your environment.

Disk provisioning is the process of creating a new disk or set of disks for a virtual machine. Disk provisioning can occur when creating a new virtual machine, adding a new drive to an existing virtual machine, cloning an existing virtual machine, or using Storage vMotion (svMotion) on a virtual machine. Each type of disk provisioning has its own advantages and disadvantages that are discussed in this section.

Change the Provisioning Type

If you need to change the provisioning type of a drive, you can do so by performing an svMotion on the virtual machine. During this process, you can change the location and provisioning type of each drive on the virtual machine. There are other ways to change the provisioning type, such as performing a virtual-to-virtual conversion of the virtual machine, but using svMotion is the easiest.

Disk Zeroing

Disk zeroing is the process of changing each bit on a storage drive to a zero to make sure that no old data exists on the disk. Disk zeroing takes time. If the zeroing is performed when the disk is created, it will take significantly longer to be added to the virtual machine but the drive will have slightly faster performance. If disk zeroing is performed during write operations on a live drive, it can slow the performance of the drive.

Thick Provisioning

Thick provisioning is the process of creating a new hard disk for a virtual machine in which all of the space is fully allocated when it is created. A thick provisioned drive is very much like a physical disk on a regular server. The disk is installed, and all the space on the disk is available and allocated during the provisioning process.

Thick Provision Eager Zeroed

Thick provision eager zeroed is a type of disk provisioning in which the entire drive is allocated and zeroed when it is initially created. Since the disk space is fully allocated and zeroed during provisioning, thick provision eager zeroed disks will give the best performance when they are used. Unfortunately, it takes some time for the disk to be zeroed, so creating a large thick provision eager zeroed drive takes longer than the other types of drives.

Imagine using thick provision eager zeroed if a 100 GB drive is created for a virtual machine. It would immediately use 100 GB on the datastore, and the entire 100 GB would be set to consecutive zeros.

The advantages and disadvantages are as follows:

Advantage

- Best performance for the virtual machine after it has been created

Disadvantage

- Takes the longest time to create

Thick Provision Lazy Zeroed

Thick provision lazy zeroed is the default disk-provisioning type. With it, the entire drive is allocated when it is initially created but is not zeroed until it is used. Since a thick provision lazy zeroed drive is zeroed as it is used, it can be created quickly but gives slightly poorer performance than a thick provision eager zeroed drive.

Imagine using thick provision lazy zeroed if a 100 GB drive is created for a virtual machine. It would immediately use 100 GB on the datastore, but the 100 GB would not be zeroed until each block on the drive is used. It would be zeroed one block at a time as each block is used.

Here are the advantages and disadvantages:

Advantages

- Slightly better performance for the virtual machine than thin provisioned drives
- Takes less time to create than thick provision eager zeroed drives

Disadvantage

- Requires disk zeroing to be performed as disk writes are being performed, causing poorer performance than thick provision eager zeroed drives

 If you are going to use thick provisioned drives, I recommend using thick provision eager zeroed drives. The additional time that it takes to create a thick provision eager zeroed vs. a thick provision lazy zeroed drive is minimal, and eager zeroed drives provide better write performance.

Thin Provisioning

Thin provisioning is a type of disk provisioning in which the entire space of the drive is not allocated when it is initially created but is allocated and zeroed as each block is used. These drives are referred to as *thin* since they do not initially take up much space on the datastore where they reside. These drives start out very small and grow as they are used up to the full allocated size of the drive.

Imagine using thin provisioning when a 100 GB drive is created for a virtual machine. It would initially not use any space on the datastore but would grow a block at a time as storage is used by the virtual machine. The drive will continue to grow and be zeroed one block at a time until it reaches 100 GB. Since thin provisioned drives take up the space only on the datastore they are actually using, they help reduce wasted space on underused virtual machine drives.

The advantages and disadvantages are as follows:

Advantage

- Allows overprovisioning of datastores, which helps reduce wasted space on virtual machines

Disadvantage

- Poorer performance than both thick provision eager zeroed and thick provision lazy zeroed drives

WARNING
Thin provisioned drives can help reduce wasted drive space and save money by reducing the need to purchase additional storage, but they can also be dangerous. If you are using thin provisioned drives, you must actively monitor your overprovisioned datastores to make sure they never run out of disk space. If a datastore becomes completely full, any virtual machine that has a thin provisioned drive on it can become nonresponsive.

By allowing datastores to be overprovisioned, thin provisioned drives can help companies save money by reducing wasted disk space. Thin provisioning can be a good choice for environments that can afford a very small performance hit. Many companies will allow thin provisioning of drives in the following circumstances:

- Test environments
- Lab environments
- Noncritical quality assurance (QA) or production environments

 Real World Scenario

Achieving Cost Savings via Thin Provisioning

One of my largest clients was experiencing a storage problem. The speed at which this company's virtual environment was consuming storage was increasing, and company officials feared that it would become unsustainable if they didn't make some changes. I worked with a team that performed an audit of the storage, and we found that the vast majority of the storage allocated to their virtual machines was not being used. The virtual machines had been created with drives that were far larger than needed and on average were only 30 percent used for data drives and 55 percent used for system drives. The company was able to institute new build procedures that called for smaller data drives that could be extended later if needed and was able to greatly slow its rate of storage consumption. We were also able to convince the company to allow the drives on new test and QA servers to be thin provisioned and for existing test and QA servers to be converted to thin provision. The conversion process enabled the company to reclaim more than 50 percent of the storage that had been allocated to its test and QA servers and allowed it to cancel several large storage orders. This resulted in significant savings in storage costs.

VMware Virtual Storage Technologies

This section describes some of the VMware technologies and products that help us leverage and manage virtual storage. By the end of the section, you will have a better understanding of these products and technologies and be able to answer questions about them for the exam. You should also be able to start identifying products you might be interested in trying in your own virtual environment. Much of this section should feel like a review of material from previous chapters.

High Availability   High availability (HA) is a VMware technology that is used to automatically restart virtual machines on a different ESXi host if the ESXi host they are on fails. Even though the virtual machines experience an outage while they are restarted, it is a much shorter outage than if the machines had to be manually restarted. This can be extremely important if an ESXi host fails in the middle of the night, when no administrators are available. HA would not be considered a disaster-recovery or disaster-tolerance solution since it is likely that in the event of a disaster multiple ESXi hosts and the shared storage they rely on would not be available.

Storage vMotion   Storage vMotion (svMotion) is a VMware technology that allows running virtual machines to be migrated from one storage location to another without experiencing any downtime. In order for this technology to work correctly, both storage locations must be accessible by the ESXi host on which the virtual machine resides.

Storage DRS   Storage DRS (SDRS) is a VMware technology that load balances virtual machine storage demand across datastores to remove the problem of hot spots, whereby one datastore is overused while others go underused. SDRS is also used to place new virtual machines onto the least heavily used datastore. SDRS uses svMotion to move virtual machines from one datastore to another.

Storage I/O Control   Storage I/O Control (SIOC) is a VMware technology that allows the storage traffic of certain virtual machines to be prioritized. It can be used to give a single virtual machine greater access to storage resources than other virtual machines on the same storage.

vSphere Storage Appliance   The vSphere Storage Appliance (VSA) is a VMware technology that can be used to aggregate unused disks on ESXi hosts and use them as shared storage. This can help bring shared storage to smaller environments where it would not be cost-effective otherwise and to branch offices of larger organizations. Many VMware technologies require shared storage, and the VSA can enable smaller organizations to use them.

vSphere Replication   vSphere Replication is a hardware-independent technology that allows running virtual machines to be replicated to another site. If a disaster were to happen to the original site, the replica virtual machine could be brought up at the other site. vSphere Replication would be considered a small-scale disaster-recovery/disaster-tolerance solution since it is used to bring back smaller sections of the environment after a smaller disaster.

Site Recovery Manager   Site Recovery Manager (SRM) is a VMware full-scale disaster-recovery/disaster-tolerance solution that can restore an entire data center with the pressing of a few buttons. It also allows live testing of the disaster-recovery plan and encourages the development of detailed disaster-recovery plans. It allows full isolation of the test environment so tests can be conducted while the production environments are still up and running.

VM Storage Profiles   VM storage profiles enable VMware datastores to be separated into different performance classes, depending on the datastore characteristics, which are based on the information provided by the storage array. VM storage profiles are then able to automatically use Storage vMotion to move virtual machine disks to the performance class of storage array on which it would perform best.

Summary

In this chapter, we discussed the types of storage that are available for use in our virtual environments. We started by covering the differences between physical and virtual storage. We then looked at shared storage and discussed how important it is to VMware. We finished the section by reviewing the VMware features that depend on shared storage to operate correctly: Distributed Power Management, high availability, Storage Distributed Resource Scheduler, Storage vMotion, VM storage profiles, and vMotion.

We then looked at the storage types that are supported by VMware. We started by talking about local storage and Fibre Channel storage. Next we looked at iSCSI and Network File System (NFS). We ended the section by briefly discussing raw device mappings (RDMs).

In the next section, we discussed the Virtual Machine File System. We started by defining VMFS and the advantages of using it. The section ended by comparing the Virtual Machine File System to the Network File System.

The next section was all about disk provisioning. We started with the definition of disk provisioning and then moved on to look at the three types of disk provisioning provided by VMware: thick provision eager zeroed, thick provision lazy zeroed, and finally thin provision. We looked at the advantages and disadvantages of each of these types of disk provisioning and ended the section by discussing some of the usage cases for thin provisioning.

In the final section of this chapter, we reviewed VMware technologies and products that help us leverage and manage our storage environment.

Exam Essentials

Understand physical storage.   Physical storage is the underlying physical hardware that provides storage to the virtual environment.

Understand virtual storage.   Virtual storage is an abstract view of the storage that is available to the virtual environment presented to the ESXi hosts.

Understand shared storage.   Shared storage is storage that is available to multiple ESXi hosts at the same time.

Know which VMware features require shared storage to operate.   The following VMware technologies require shared storage to operate: Distributed Power Management, high availability, Storage Distributed Resource Scheduler, Storage vMotion, VM storage profiles, and vMotion.

Understand the available VMware storage types.   The following are available storage types for VMware environments: local storage, Fibre Channel, iSCSI, and the Network File System.

Know the advantages of using local storage.   Local storage is easy to configure, relatively inexpensive, and can make installation of ESXi hosts less complicated.

Know the disadvantages of using local storage.   Local storage cannot be configured as a raw device mapping. High availability cannot be used for virtual machines stored on local storage.

Know the advantages of using Fibre Channel storage.   Fibre Channel storage provides very high performance and allows boot-from-SAN.

Know the disadvantages of using Fibre Channel storage.   Fibre Channel storage is difficult to configure, very expensive, and requires additional hardware to be added to the ESXi hosts.

Know the advantages of using iSCSI storage.   iSCSI storage is relatively easy to configure, less expensive than Fibre Channel, and allows boot-from-SAN.

Know the disadvantages of using iSCSI storage.   iSCSI storage provides lesser performance than Fibre Channel and requires additional network cards to be added to the ESXi hosts.

Know the advantages of using Network File System (NFS) storage.   NFS storage is easy to configure and inexpensive when compared to other shared storage options.

Know the disadvantages of using Network File System (NFS) storage.   NFS storage does not support the VMFS and provides lesser performing storage performance.

Understand raw device mappings.   A raw device mapping (RDM) is a virtual drive pointer in VMware that points to a raw physical storage device.

Understand the Virtual Machine File System.   The Virtual Machine File System is a high-performance file system designed by VMware that allows multiple ESXi hosts to have read-write access to the file system at the same time and is optimized for virtual machines.

Understand disk provisioning.   Disk provisioning is the process of creating a new disk or set of disks for a virtual machine.

Understand disk zeroing.   Disk zeroing is the process of changing each bit on a storage drive to a zero to make sure that no old data exists on the disk.

Understand thick provision eager zeroed disks.   Thick provision eager zeroed is a type of disk provisioning in which the entire drive is allocated and zeroed when it is initially created.

Know the advantages and disadvantages of using thick provision eager zeroed disks.   Thick provision eager zeroed disks provide the best performance for the virtual machine after it has been created but take the longest time to create.

Know the advantages and disadvantages of using thick provision lazy zeroed disks.   Thick provision lazy zeroed disks provide slightly better performance for the virtual machine than thin provision drives and take a shorter time to create than thick provision eager zeroed drives. However, thick provision lazy zeroed disks require disk zeroing to be performed concurrently with disk writes, causing poorer performance than thick provision eager zeroed drives.

Know the advantages and disadvantages of using thin provision disks.   Thin provision disks allow overprovisioning of datastores, which helps reduce wasted space on virtual machines, but they provide poorer performance than both thick provision eager zeroed and thick provision lazy zeroed drives.

Understand the usage cases for thin provision disks.   Thin provision disks are used in test environments, lab environments, and noncritical QA or production environments.

Know which VMware features are used to manage or leverage storage in a VMware environment.   The following VMware products are used to manage or leverage storage in a VMware environment: high availability, Storage vMotion, Storage DRS, Storage I/O Control, vSphere Storage Appliance, vSphere Replication, Site Recovery Manager, and VM storage profiles.

Review Questions

You can find the answers in Appendix A.

1. Which of the following is best described as the underlying hardware that provides storage to the virtual environment?

   A. Physical storage

   B. Virtual storage

   C. Shared storage

   D. Both A and C

2. Which of the following VMware technologies moves virtual machines from one datastore to another?

   A. vMotion

   B. Storage vMotion

   C. VM storage profiles

   D. Both B and C

3. Which of the following is not an advantage of using local storage in a VMware environment?

   A. Local storage is easy to configure.

   B. Local storage is relatively inexpensive.

   C. Local storage can be easily shared across ESXi hosts.

   D. Local storage can make the installation of ESXi hosts less complicated.

4. What is the purpose of disk zeroing?

   A. To expand a drive to its full size

   B. To format an old drive for reuse

   C. To delete a file from a drive

   D. To make sure that no data exists on a new disk or disk block

5. Which of the following VMware storage types uses a standard network connection to connect an ESXi host to external shared storage?

   A. Fibre Channel

   B. iSCSI

   C. Network File System (NFS)

   D. Both B and C

6. Which of the following disk provision types provides the best write performance during production?

   A. Thick provision eager zeroed

   B. Thick provision lazy zeroed

   C. Thick provision fully zeroed

   D. Thin provision

7. Which of the following allows a virtual machine to connect directly to a physical storage device?

   A. Raw device mapping

   B. Network File System

   C. Fibre Channel

   D. iSCSI

8. Which of the following VMware technologies can be used to clear a datastore before performing maintenance on it?

   A. Storage vMotion

   B. Storage DRS

   C. High availability

   D. None of the above

9. Which of the following is the least ideal usage case for thin provisioned drives?

   A. Virtual machines in a test environment

   B. Virtual machines in a critical high-performance production environment

   C. Virtual machines in a noncritical production environment

   D. Virtual machines in a quality assurance (QA) environment

10. During which of the following operations can the disk provisioning of a drive not be set or changed?

    A. When the drive is created

    B. When an existing virtual machine is cloned

    C. When using vMotion

    D. When using Storage vMotion (svMotion)

11. Which of the following is a file system designed by VMware to be optimized for virtual machines?

    A. iSCSI

    B. NFS

    C. VMFS

    D. Fibre Channel

12. Which of the following disk provision types is the default for new drives?

    A. Thick provision eager zeroed.

    B. Thick provision lazy zeroed.

    C. Thin provision.

    D. None of these is the default.

13. Which of the following disk provision types takes the longest to add to a virtual machine?

    A. Thick provision eager zeroed

    B. Thick provision lazy zeroed

    C. Thick provision fully zeroed

    D. Thin provision

14. Which of the following is best described as an abstracted view of the storage that is available in the VMware environment?

    A. Physical storage

    B. Virtual storage

    C. Shared storage

    D. Network File System (NFS)

15. Which of the following VMware technologies uses vMotion to move virtual machines from one ESXi host to another?

    A. Storage vMotion

    B. Storage DRS

    C. High availability

    D. None of the above

16. Which of the following disk provision types consumes all the space on the datastore that is allocated to it when the drive is created?

    A. Thick provision eager zeroed

    B. Thick provision lazy zeroed

    C. Thin provision

    D. Both A and B

17. Which of the following storage types require special cards called host bus adapters to be installed on the ESXi hosts?

    A. Local storage

    B. Fibre Channel

    C. iSCSI

    D. Network File System

18. Which of the following VMware products would be considered a disaster-recovery technology?

    A. The vSphere Storage Appliance

    B. Site Recovery Manager

    C. VM storage profiles

    D. Storage DRS

19. Which of the following VMware technologies is used by Distributed Power Management to migrate virtual machines off an ESXi host before it is powered down?

    A. Storage Distributed Resource Scheduler

    B. High availability

    C. vMotion

    D. Storage vMotion

20. Which of the following is best described as storage that is available to multiple ESXi hosts at the same time?

    A. Physical storage

    B. Virtual storage

    C. Shared storage

    D. Network File System

Chapter

5

Networking in a VMware Environment

THE VCA-DCV TOPICS COVERED IN THIS CHAPTER INCLUDE THE FOLLOWING:

✓ **Differentiate vSphere networking technologies**

- ▪ Differentiate physical and virtual networking
- ▪ Differentiate VMware virtual switch technologies
- ▪ Identify VMware virtual switch components
- ▪ Identify common virtual switch policies
- ▪ Identify capabilities of Network I/O Control

This chapter discusses networking in a VMware environment. You will learn about physical and virtual switches—what they are and what they can do. The chapter covers VMware virtual switch technologies that are available and how to identify VMware virtual switch components. It also covers common virtual switch policies and the capabilities of Network I/O Control. By the end of this chapter, you should have an understanding of not only how networking works in a VMware environment, but also some advanced networking concepts that leverage network virtualization.

Differentiate Physical and Virtual Networking

This section presents some of the differences between physical switches and VMware virtual switches.

Physical Switches

Let's start by looking at a physical switch and its properties:

- Fixed number of network cable connections (ports) to other switches, routers, or physical servers
- Dynamically keeps track of MAC addresses connected to it
- Can provide Layer 2 or possibly Layer 3 switching

When you buy a new physical switch, usually you pay for the ports. This means that the more connections you need, the more expensive it is. And after you buy the switch, there is no changing the number of ports.

When you start talking about physical switches, it is helpful to have an understanding of the abstraction provided by the layer model. When you hear the term *layers*, this is usually a reference to the Open Systems Interconnection (OSI) communication model. In all, this model has seven layers. Layer 1 is the physical media the network runs on. It is unlikely that you will encounter any questions on the layers of the OSI model. However, if you are researching anything networking related, it will be beneficial to know about these. Each layer of the OSI model builds on the previous layer. Using layers, an application has to deal with only the top layer of networking. Here are all seven of the layers:

7	Application	High-level APIs that programs can use
6	Presentation	Application and networking service translation
5	Session	Manages communication sessions (for example, FTP session)
4	Transport	Transmission protocol (for example, RDP)
3	Network	Addressing, routing, and controlling traffic
2	Data-Link	Data frame transmission
1	Physical	Raw streams over physical medium

Physical network switches keep track of MAC addresses so that the switch can route network traffic. The physical switch keeps an index of MAC addresses to ports in memory. The switch does this for all the locally attached devices on its local ports as well as remote devices connected through to other switches.

Think of a small network with a dozen servers connected to one physical switch. Each one of the servers has at least one network card, and every network card has a MAC address. Let's say you have two domain controllers, named DC1 and DC2. If domain controller DC1 wants to talk to DC2, DC1 sends a TCP packet out the network interface on the server. The physical switch takes the packet and adds the source MAC address and the port to its dynamic index in memory. Then the switch looks up the destination MAC address in its table in memory, finds DC2, and sends the packet along.

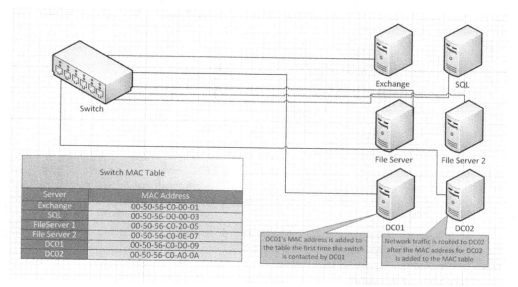

You may ask how the physical network switch knows about DC2 in this scenario. Here's how: if the physical switch does not have the destination MAC address in its internal table in memory, it will send the packet from DC1 to all ports on the physical switch except for the port DC1 is plugged into. The switch does this to learn what port to use to forward traffic. If a server or device has the MAC address the switch is looking for, the switch will see a response from the device on a specific port. It will use this information going forward by updating the table in memory. If DC1 is on a different physical switch than DC2, and the switches are connected, the same process is followed. That means both physical switches will remember the MAC addresses of both servers to route between them.

Virtual Switches

First things first—when you create a new virtual switch through the vSphere or web client, you have to choose what you want to use the virtual switch for. Virtual machine traffic or VMkernel traffic are your two choices. If you know you want to use this new switch for the management console, iSCSI, NFS, or vMotion, you choose VMkernel. If you know you want to use the new switch for routing typical virtual machine network traffic, choose Virtual Machine.

 The VMware world uses two types of switches: standard virtual switches and distributed switches. An Enterprise Plus license is required to set up distributed switches, and distributed switches are much easier to manage when you have a lot of hosts. With distributed switches, configuration of each ESXi host can be automatic. See the "Differentiate VMware Virtual Switch Technologies" section later in this chapter.

Now let's look at a standard virtual switch that steps in for a physical switch. Assuming all the physical servers are now virtualized and residing on a host with the hypervisor (ESXi) installed, here are some virtual switch properties:

- Knows what MAC address is connected to each port
- Has an expandable number of ports
- Requires port groups to connect to virtual machines
- Routes communication for VMkernel traffic
- Usually connects to an uplink port for off-host traffic
- Handles layer 2 networking switch

The standard virtual switch (vSwitch) knows what MAC address is connected to each port. The virtual switch does *not* broadcast MAC addresses to all connected ports to learn MAC addresses. Also the virtual switch does not keep track of the MAC addresses of any nonlocal devices.

The virtual switch has an expandable number of ports, with a maximum of 4,088 ports. However, the number of ports on a virtual switch is not configurable with ESXi 5.5. The number of ports is dynamic and will automatically expand as the need arises. This is a big deal and is a distinct advantage of virtual switches.

A virtual switch supports a large number of ports (4,088). However, other configuration maximums can prevent you from using all 4,088 ports at once. In fact, the maximum number of active ports per host is only 1,016. The number of ports on a virtual switch is dynamic and adjusts automatically. Also remember that ports are used for tasks other than virtual machine traffic. In fact, every virtual switch uses eight ports that are reserved for network discovery and management.

A virtual switch requires port groups to connect to virtual machines. When a virtual machine is created, you specify the port group to use for networking. By default, the network will be assigned to a default virtual machine traffic port group. Multiple virtual machines can use the same port group.

A port group routes communication for VMkernel traffic. Port groups can be used for virtual machine network traffic or for VMkernel traffic. Tasks like the management network, vMotion, and iSCSI use a VMkernel port group. Figure 5.1 shows a snippet of port groups from the host configuration properties' Networking section as an example.

FIGURE 5.1   These are all standard switches.

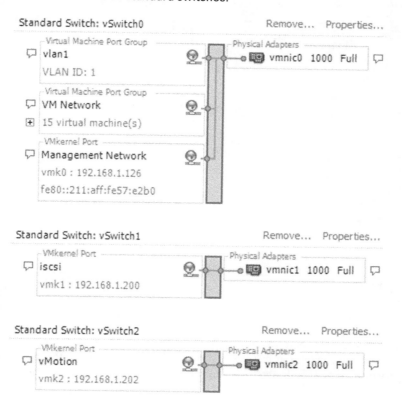

Notice on the right side, you see physical adapters. A port group usually connects to an uplink port for off-host traffic. The uplink is used by virtual machines to talk to the physical network. A physical network card, or uplink, is not required for a port group. However, virtual machines connected to a port group without an uplink port will be able to communicate only with virtual machines on the same host.

If a port group has more than one network card added as an uplink, you can do some interesting things. You can increase the aggregate speed of the port group or assign a network card as a standby adapter for failover during primary network card failure (see Figure 5.2).

FIGURE 5.2   Port groups—multiple network cards

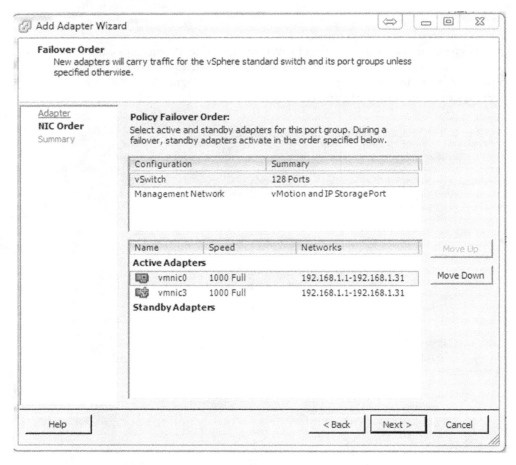

A virtual switch on an ESXi host is a layer 2 network switch. *Layer 2* refers to the seven-layer OSI networking model. Layer 2 is the Data-Link layer, just above the layer 1 Physical layer (the network card). It is doubtful any OSI questions, including layer 2 questions, will be on the test.

Differences Between Physical and Virtual Switches

Virtual switches have a lot in common with physical switches. Before getting into differences, let's see what some of those similarities are. Both physical and virtual switches route network traffic for servers. Virtual switches route the same kind of packets that physical switches do. Routing traffic between two servers connected to the same switch, physical or virtual, is done by MAC address. Both types of switches keep track of the MAC addresses of devices connected directly to it.

So, the similarities between physical and virtual switches are kind of obvious. Both route network packets. Both keep track of MAC addresses. And both can connect to various devices. However, there are some important differences between physical switches and virtual switches.

One of the biggest differences between a physical switch and a standard virtual switch is tracking of the MAC addresses of connected devices. Imagine a virtual machine sending network traffic to a physical server on the network. The network packet would go to the virtual switch, looking for a MAC address that the virtual switch knows nothing about. The virtual switch just hands off the network packet to the uplink. When the response comes back from the physical server, the virtual switch does not record the MAC address of the physical server. This is different from a physical switch. A physical switch would track the MAC address of the physical server.

The number of ports on a physical switch is fixed. The number of ports on a virtual switch is automatically expandable: the virtual switch will dynamically adjust the number of ports used as resources are needed—at least, up to a point. The maximum number of ports is 4,096 minus 8 reserved ports (4,088) for each ESXi host.

Security, traffic shaping, and NIC teaming properties are available in the virtual switch properties. Also, virtual switches are layer 2 switches. Physical switches can be layer 2 or layer 3. Layer 3 switches are smarter. The higher the layer a switch can handle, the smarter the switch is. Layer 2 switching is at the frame level. Layer 3 switching is at the network level and can handle path determination and logical addressing.

Differentiate VMware Virtual Switch Technologies

This section covers the two virtual switch technologies available from VMware and some of the advantages of each.

The first virtual switch type is the standard virtual switch, also known as the *vSwitch*. The other is the distributed virtual switch, also known as the *dvSwitch*.

The vNetwork Distributed Switch is also known as the vDS, the distributed virtual switch, and dvSwitch.

Standard Virtual Switches

The standard virtual switch is created on each host. It handles basic network communication between virtual machines on the same or other hosts, as well as communications between virtual machines and the physical network. A virtual switch can have multiple port groups assigned to it. The port groups connected to a virtual switch do not all have to be of the same type. You can have a virtual machine network port group connected to the same vSwitch as a VMkernel port group, for instance.

> The standard virtual switch can be created without vCenter. This is one of the biggest differences between the standard virtual switch and the distributed virtual switch. You need a vCenter Server license in order to run vCenter and leverage the vNetwork Distributed Switch.

A standard switch can be used for normal virtual machine traffic, or VMkernel traffic such as management, vMotion, and NFS. If you have only a couple of ESXi hosts, a standard switch may be all you need. Imagine you have a small virtual environment with three ESXi hosts and 40 virtual machines. You have domain controllers, Exchange servers, SQL servers, application servers, and file servers. Of course, you want to leverage vMotion and have a SAN backend.

When you configure the virtual switches, you create a vMotion port group as well as a virtual machine network port. You name the port groups consistently across all three hosts. You have to create the port groups three times, once on each host—not too difficult when you have only three hosts.

Port Group Names

When you create a new port group, you have to give it a name. If you are relying on standard virtual switches and plan to use vMotion, the name of the port group used for vMotion must be the same on every host. And the name is case sensitive. It is critical that new hosts added to the cluster have port groups configured identically if you want to leverage vMotion.

Distributed Virtual Switches

A distributed virtual switch is a very different beast from a standard virtual switch. Distributed virtual switches can do everything that standard virtual switches can do and more. Distributed virtual switches require higher-level licenses. You need Enterprise Plus licensing for vSphere to create a distributed virtual switch.

Distributed virtual switches are usually used in large environments where you have a lot of hosts. To create a distributed virtual switch, you need vCenter Server. After you create the switch, vCenter Server does the work to configure each host in a cluster. This makes the configuration of each host consistent. When you have a lot of hosts, this is a big deal.

 Real World Scenario

Transitions

Distributed virtual switches are a very good idea. You really learn this lesson when you experience serious problems with VMware and realize that a distributed port group would have prevented the problem in the first place. I learned this when we started expanding VMware clusters and had to manually type in more than a dozen port groups. One person mistypes, uses the wrong case, or misspells the port group, and suddenly, vMotion no longer works. I ended up writing a PowerShell script to create all of the networking settings on each new ESXi host to guarantee consistency. Then the network changes, which means every ESXi host will need to be modified. And, distributed switches comes to the rescue!

Some features in distributed switches make troubleshooting network issues easier. Network administrators used to have limited visibility into internal virtual machine networking. With industry standard tools such as port mirroring (gets a complete copy of all traffic on a port) and NetFlow (monitors network traffic), network administrators can troubleshoot network issues in virtual machines the same way they do with physical switches and routers. Let's look at some of the other features of distributed switches:

- Network Health Check
- Bidirectional traffic filtering
- Link aggregation
- Backup and restore
- Distributed virtual port groups
- Distributed virtual uplinks
- Private VLANs
- Network vMotion
- Third-party virtual switch support

Network Health Check will automatically check some network settings at regular intervals. Parameters for the VLAN, MTU, and adapter teaming are checked, and if a configuration problem is detected, a warning is generated.

Network Parameters

Using VLANs is a way to have network segments that are mapped logically instead of physically. Devices on isolated physical segments can communicate as if they are on the same segment. VLANs are very prominent in today's networks.

MTU is the Maximum Transmission Unit, a parameter that defines how big of a chunk of data a device can handle at a time.

Adapter Teaming is a way to bridge two network adapters together seamlessly so that you can leverage the combined bandwidth instead of each network connection individually. Adapter Teaming can also be used in a failover fashion so that when one network connection fails, the other network connection takes over seamlessly.

Bidirectional traffic filtering is used to filter traffic. Sounds fairly simple and straightforward, I know. This feature enhances security and is sometimes referred to as access control lists (ACLs). This is basically the same thing routers provide, and packets can be filtered or tagged. You can filter on MAC addresses, IP addresses, or type of traffic (for example, vMotion). And, of course, filtering can be done in both directions.

Link aggregation is banding network connections together to realize a larger capacity. Distributed switches support this feature via the Link Aggregation Control Protocol. This protocol provides load-balancing algorithms, support for link aggregate groups, and configuration templates.

Backup and restore brings peace of mind that you can recover from a catastrophe and restore your network configuration. This was more of a problem with previous versions of the distributed virtual switch.

Distributed virtual port groups provide abstraction for the port groups on each host. This allows you to push configuration options to all port groups in a dvSwitch.

Distributed virtual uplinks also provide abstraction for a dvSwitch, but for the virtual uplinks on each host.

Private VLANs provide advancement over regular VLANs. A regular VLAN is a way to segment a broadcast network domain. Private VLANs provide a way to further segment a regular VLAN.

Network vMotion is like an advanced vMotion. That is, policies and the network state of a virtual machine are maintained through the Network vMotion process. There is no special Network vMotion option; you perform a normal vMotion operation, and the stats and policies are maintained.

Third-party virtual switch support provides hooks for third-party products such as Cisco's Nexus 1000V and IBM's 5000V.

 It is helpful for the exam to understand the concept of distributed virtual switches. However, you will not find most of the advanced concepts on the test. These are included for completeness.

Identify VMware Virtual Switch Components

In this section, you'll get more exposure to virtual switches as we expand on their components. We will break this down by standard virtual switches and distributed virtual switches.

Standard Virtual Switch

A virtual switch has a direct connection to the virtual network interface card on a virtual machine. A virtual switch also has a direct connection to the physical network interface card (NIC) on the physical host running VMware ESXi (through the hypervisor). A virtual machine that wants to talk to anything over the physical or virtual network must be connected to a virtual switch. Figure 5.3 shows what a standard virtual switch looks like.

FIGURE 5.3   Standard switch

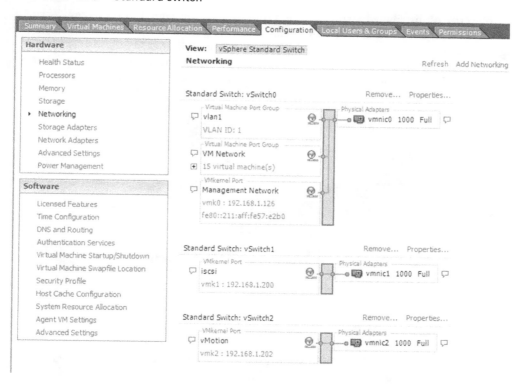

Standard virtual switches take the place of physical switches and are made up of a few components:

- Virtual ports
- Port groups
- Uplinks

Virtual ports are what each virtual machine connects to, assuming the virtual machine will talk on the network. A virtual port would connect to the virtual network interface card that is installed in the virtual machine operating system.

Port groups can be VMkernel or virtual machine ports. VMkernel ports are used for networking things like iSCSI, vMotion, NFS, and management of the virtual switch. Virtual machine ports are used for general networking on the virtual machine.

Uplinks are virtual ports but are used for connection to the physical world by way of a physical NIC. They are on the right-hand side of the screen in the vSphere client's host networking configuration (see Figure 5.4).

Distributed Virtual Switch

One objective of distributed virtual switches is to manage the aggregate resources, combined on all hosts, the same way you manage the resources of a VMware cluster: by aggregating the CPU, memory, and network resources of all hosts.

Distributed virtual switches are a little different from standard virtual switches. That is, they have dvUplinks in place of uplinks. And the port groups are called dvPortGroups. Figure 5.4 shows a typical dvSwitch.

FIGURE 5.4   dvSwitch

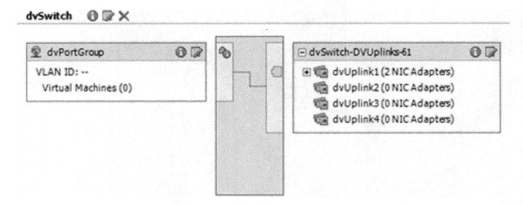

Both a dvPortGroup and a standard port group are used to add networking. When you assign a network port group for a virtual machine, you can select the dvPortGroup via the drop-down in the vSphere client (see Figure 5.5). dvUplinks provide a way to abstract the uplinks available on the hosts in a distributed virtual switch.

FIGURE 5.5   Selecting the port group

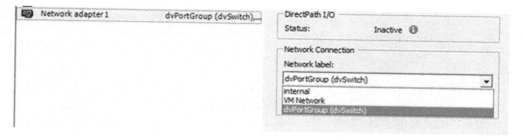

 If you are starting with a simple VMware environment and you might expand things in the future, you should buy extra network interface cards on new hosts so that you can migrate to distributed virtual switches with less effort. You can assign extra cards as active standbys or for network teaming; you may also want to add fault tolerance to an existing cluster. Fault tolerance requires dedicated network interface cards.

Identify Common Virtual Switch Policies

Just as virtual switches come in two forms, standard and distributed, virtual switch polices do as well: (standard) port group policies and distributed virtual switch policies. This section covers these two types and the advantages each one provides.

Port Group Policies

Port group policies are applied on standard virtual switches. Basic networking configuration settings are here. Check the properties of any port group contained in a vSwitch and you can see what default policies are available. Remember that there may be more than one port group on each standard virtual switch. When you are modifying the standard virtual switch policies, you have to do the work on each port group. If there are three port groups that make up a standard virtual switch, and you want to modify the settings for the entire standard virtual switch, you will need to make the changes on each of the port groups.

Figure 5.6 shows the properties of a port group.

FIGURE 5.6   Port group properties and effective policies

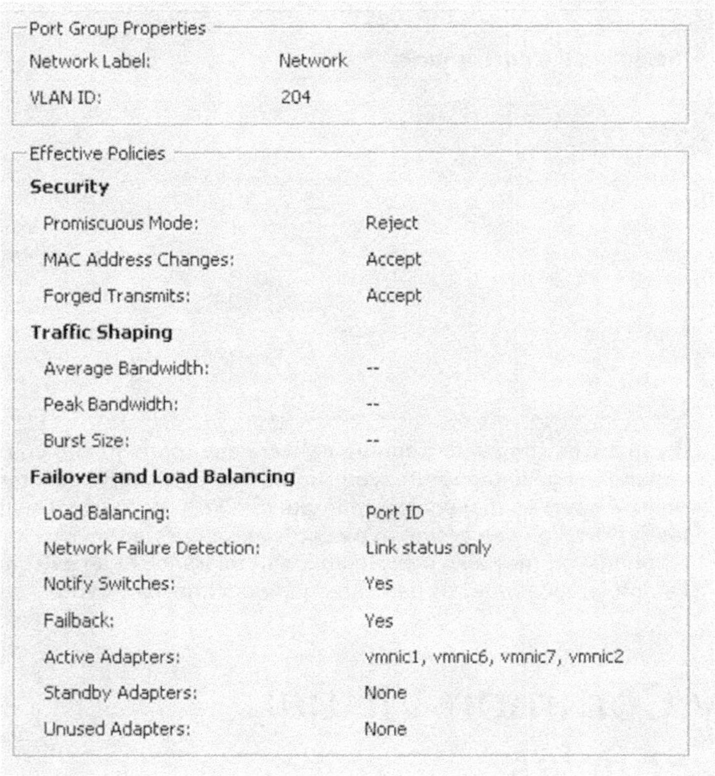

```
┌─ Port Group Properties ─────────────────────────────────────────┐
│  Network Label:              Network                             │
│  VLAN ID:                    204                                 │
└─────────────────────────────────────────────────────────────────┘

┌─ Effective Policies ────────────────────────────────────────────┐
│  Security                                                        │
│    Promiscuous Mode:            Reject                           │
│    MAC Address Changes:         Accept                           │
│    Forged Transmits:            Accept                           │
│  Traffic Shaping                                                 │
│    Average Bandwidth:           --                               │
│    Peak Bandwidth:              --                               │
│    Burst Size:                  --                               │
│  Failover and Load Balancing                                    │
│    Load Balancing:              Port ID                          │
│    Network Failure Detection:   Link status only                │
│    Notify Switches:             Yes                              │
│    Failback:                    Yes                              │
│    Active Adapters:             vmnic1, vmnic6, vmnic7, vmnic2   │
│    Standby Adapters:            None                             │
│    Unused Adapters:             None                             │
└─────────────────────────────────────────────────────────────────┘
```

You can set the network label as well as the VLAN ID in the port group properties (top). There are three configurable sections under Effective Policies: Security, Traffic Shaping, and Failover and Load Balancing. Let's break each of these down.

Security

There are several security related settings that have usable defaults, although it is nice to know these are here when you need them.

Promiscuous Mode   You can set this to Accept or Reject. Many people enable this mode so that network packet captures can be run on virtual machines. This setting lets the virtual machine network cards see all of the network traffic on the virtual wire. This is exactly the same as a physical network card in a physical server, which needs to be in promiscuous mode to capture traffic on the network. Both VMkernel and virtual machine port groups have these settings. Setting promiscuous mode to Reject is a way to prevent traffic sniffing.

MAC Address Changes   You can set this to Accept or Reject. This setting controls whether an operating system running on a virtual machine can change the MAC address. All virtual network adapters connected to virtual machines have a MAC address generated for them. If an operating system tries to change the MAC address, it could be trying to intercept network traffic meant for another virtual machine. Setting this to Reject will prevent this from happening.

MAC Changes and iSCSI

Rejecting MAC changes on a virtual port group will stop some forms of network hacking. However, some services require the operating system be able to change the MAC address. For example, iSCSI may need to be able to change the effective MAC address in order to function. Also load balancing that uses Unicast mode requires multiple virtual machines to have the same MAC address.

Forged Transmits   Again, you can set this to Accept or Reject. This setting is another MAC address change policy. But this time, the port group policy is looking at the effective MAC address compared to the source MAC address (not the initial MAC address). Setting this policy to Reject will prevent MAC address impersonation.

Traffic Shaping

Traffic shaping policies on standard virtual switches apply to outbound virtual switch traffic only.

Average Bandwidth   By default, traffic shaping is disabled. Traffic shaping can be directly related to average bandwidth since traffic shaping can implement resource limits. If you look at the properties of a virtual switch under the Traffic Shaping tab (see Figure 5.7), you can enable it. The default average bandwidth is 100,000 kbps. Use this to limit the average bandwidth over time.

FIGURE 5.7   Virtual switch traffic shaping

General	Security	Traffic Shaping	NIC Teaming

Policy Exceptions

Status:	Enabled ▼	
Average Bandwidth:	100000	Kbits/sec
Peak Bandwidth:	100000	Kbits/sec
Burst Size:	102400	Kbytes

ⓘ Traffic shaping policy is applied to the traffic of each virtual network adapter attached to the vSphere standard switch.

Peak Bandwidth   Peak Bandwidth limits the bandwidth while sending a burst of traffic. This one cannot be less than the average setting.

Burst Size   This limits the size of a burst of network traffic.

Failover and Load Balancing

These settings usually have to be tweaked when you first set up your VMware environment. Once you have these configured correctly, you seldom have to change them. Unless of course, your networking environment changes.

Load Balancing   This setting is used to determine how to balance traffic across adapters. You can base the load balancing on originating port ID, IP hash, MAC hash, or explicitly by order of the cards (you can move them up and down).

Network Failure Detection   This option specifies the method for determining whether a network failure occurs. The only two options are Link Status Only and Beacon Probing. Beacon Probing uses link status as well as beacon probes. Beacon Probing is like a superset, meaning link status is still used, but probing is done as well. Probing is typically used when no Link State Tracking is available on the physical switch.

Notify Switches   This setting is used to determine whether to notify switches of a failure. This is a simple Yes or No and depends on the physical switch and your environment. This setting is purely for the physical switches in your environment. Disable this when using Microsoft Network Load Balancing (NLB) in Unicast mode, since enabling this configuration setting would break the unicast NLB communication. Microsoft NLB configures all MAC addresses to be the same, so ESXi ARP updates to the physical switch would be catastrophic.

Failback   This option determines whether, after a network failure, the link will fail back to the original configuration.

Active Adapters   This setting is just as it sounds—a list of active adapters. This is where you would use the Move Up and Move Down buttons to get the priority you need.

Standby Adapters   This is a standby adapters list. These are used if there is a network adapter failure.

Unused Adapters   This lists the adapters that have not been assigned to anything. Use this for future needs or add them to virtual switches to use.

Distributed Virtual Switch Policies

Distributed virtual switch polices have similarities to standard port group policies, but with some advanced functionality, which we'll discuss here.

 All the standard virtual switch policies are available on distributed switches. In this section, we list just the advanced stuff that is not exclusive to distributed switches. Again, every policy available on the standard virtual switch is available on the distributed switch as well.

First off, to modify the policies of a distributed switch, you can use the vSphere client installed on your local workstation or the vSphere web client.

If you want to use the vSphere web client, after logging into the vCenter server (at port 9443), navigate to Home ➤ vCenter ➤ Networking. Policies for distributed switches are configured at the data center level. After selecting the data center to work on, select the port group for the distributed switch.

If you are using the local vSphere client, choose Home ➤ Inventory ➤ Networking and select the distributed switch that you want to modify.

Figure 5.8 shows the policies available on a distributed switch using the local vSphere client.

FIGURE 5.8 Managing port groups

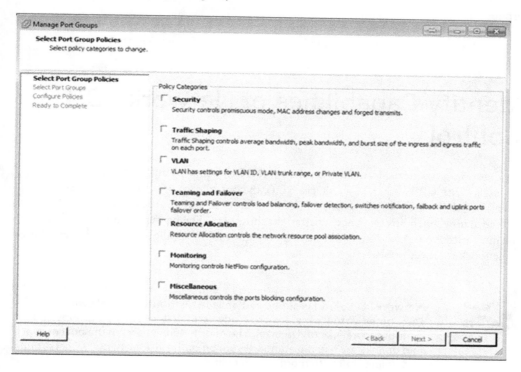

Notice there are several that are not on the standard virtual switch policies. Think of a distributed virtual switch as a superset of a standard virtual switch. The following are the policies exclusive to distributed virtual switches:

- VLAN
- Resource Allocation
- Monitoring

- Traffic Filtering and Marking is not shown in Figure 5.8. The setting is shown only in the vSphere web client.

- Miscellaneous

You can configure VLAN settings for the ID, trunk range, or private VLAN with policies for distributed switches.

Resource Allocation allows you to assign a network resource pool to a distributed port group. This could be used to give certain traffic more priority.

Monitoring is a simple setting that you can use to enable NetFlow, which is usually used for troubleshooting network issues.

Traffic Filtering and Marking allows router type functionality into your settings for distributed port groups. Just as the name says, you can filter and mark network traffic.

The Miscellaneous option simply allows you to block all ports on the distributed port group.

These are considered advanced settings, and you will most likely not see these topics on the test. However, it is always a good idea to know what your options are.

Identify Capabilities of Network I/O Control

This section introduces Network I/O Control (NIOC) concepts and configuration.

Just as with CPU and memory shares, you can control network traffic resources and assign priority. When working with CPU and memory resources, the term *shares* is a way to reference how much attention each virtual machine gets. The higher the number of shares, the more attention. And, like CPU and memory shares, NIOC allows you to allocate shares to network resource pools.

Network I/O Control is supported only on distributed virtual switches. Distributed virtual switches are made up of distributed port groups and distributed uplinks (dvUplinks). The distributed version of the port group and uplinks are like the standard version of the virtual switch's port groups and uplinks but with more functionality.

NIOC might make more sense if you look at an example of where you could leverage it. One reason NIOC is a big deal is the move to 10GbE network ports. In the old days, an ESXi server could have a lot of 1 GB network connections. These different connections would be used for different things. For example, you could have two network connections for virtual machine traffic, two network connections for management, one dedicated connection for vMotion, and one dedicated connection for NFS. Using separate adapters like this has a built-in isolation effect. For example, the vMotion network connection will not be used for virtual machine traffic.

Now, replace all those connections with a single 10GbE connection on each host. And, all of a sudden, your vMotion traffic could impact your virtual machine traffic since they are now using the same network connection. This is where you can leverage some of the NIOC features.

Let's start with the basic features:

- Isolation
- Limits
- Shares
- Teaming

When you leverage isolation, you get back what you had when you were using separate network connections for each resource. That is, you can prevent one type of traffic from impacting another by creating multiple resource pools.

You can put limits or assign shares on network resources, just as you do when you are configuring the CPU and memory restrictions.

Teaming, also known as *load-based teaming*, will allow you to more effectively use the network resource dvUplinks by spreading network load across them. This is done by configuring multiple dvUplinks to a distributed switch.

NetIOC uses traffic classes to isolate and carve up network resource pools and assign default shares. You can think of each class as tagged by what it is used for. For example, NFS traffic has a specific resource type. Here are the resource types:

- Fault tolerance—used to keep virtual machines in lock step
- iSCSI—used for virtual machines' iSCSI storage traffic
- Management—used for management traffic
- NFS—used for NFS network traffic
- Virtual machine—used for virtual machine network traffic
- vMotion—used for active vMotion processes
- vSphere Replication (VR) traffic—used for replication

 The virtual machine type defaults to 100 shares; all of the others default to 50 shares.

Now comes the fun part. You can modify the defaults any way you see fit. And you can create your own class and assign network resource pool requirements. Appropriately, these are called *user-defined network resource groups*. So if you wanted to prioritize Exchange messaging traffic to get a higher percentage of the shares, or limit the number of shares, you could do just that with NIOC. Let's go through a typical setup of NIOC.

Contention

Like CPU shares and memory shares, network resource pool groups and shares do not take effect unless there is contention with network traffic on the physical uplink for the distributed virtual switch. The good news is that, if there is no contention for the network resources, virtual machines can use more bandwidth than shares would allow. If demand from two or more virtual machines exceeds resources, there is contention.

Of course, you have to have an existing distributed virtual switch in order to enable NIOC. In the vSphere client, go to Home ➤ Inventory ➤ Networking. Click the distributed virtual switch in the tree on the left, and the Resource Allocation tab in the right pane. Then click Properties (see Figure 5.9).

FIGURE 5.9   Resource Allocation properties

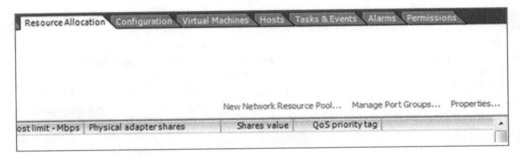

You will get a dialog box with only one option (see Figure 5.10). Select the check box and save your changes.

FIGURE 5.10   Network I/O Control

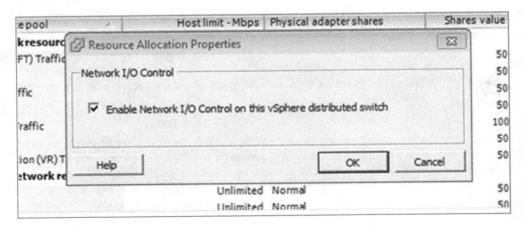

At this point, you will want to create a new resource pool for your Exchange traffic. Click the New Network Resource Pool option in the right pane to launch the dialog box (see Figure 5.11).

FIGURE 5.11   Network resource pool settings

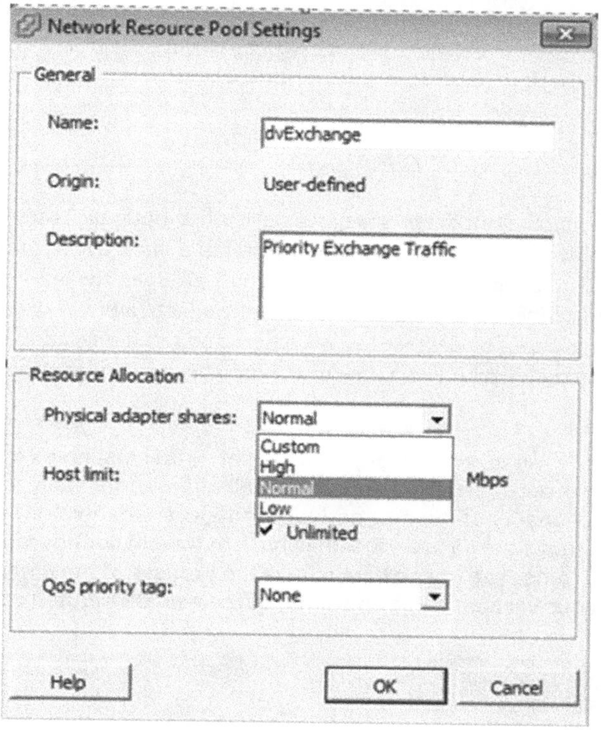

These settings allow you to name the new network resource pool and enter a description. As you can see, you have the options of Custom, High, Normal, and Low. The Low setting will give you 25 shares, Normal sets 50 shares, and High sets 100 shares. The default resource allocation shares are set at Normal. You cannot set anything above 100 shares. For our Exchange traffic, I set this one up as dvExchange, which is set to 100 shares.

By default, the host limit is set to Unlimited. Deselect the Unlimited check box to hard-code a host limit for the network resource pool. The limit is in Mbps, and the default is 10,000. The QoS priority tag is changed if you want the network traffic for the resources tagged for downstream devices such as physical switches. Tagging adds information to each packet in a network stream.

Now that we have the new network resource group, let's connect the distributed port group with the user-defined network resource pool that we created. We are using the default distributed port group, but you could create one specifically for Exchange traffic. Figure 5.12 shows the dialog box from clicking Manage Port Groups in the right pane on the Resource Allocation tab.

FIGURE 5.12   Port group association resource pool

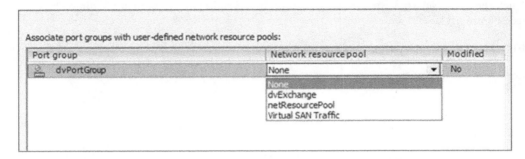

In the Network Resource Pool drop-down, we have a few options. You see the user-defined network resource pool we created: dvExchange. Select it and click OK to make the connection.

The only thing left is to assign this new distributed port group to the individual virtual machine or group of machines. There are ways to migrate a large number of virtual machines to a new distributed port group. You can use the web client and run a migration wizard. You can also drag and drop a virtual machine to a new distributed port group by using the vSphere client.

WARNING   If you plan to move a large number of virtual machines to a new distributed port group, you should move a small number manually first to verify the functionality of the new network configuration. Also remember that you can move the virtual machines back to the old configuration if you run into problems. The image here shows the process of moving a virtual machine, like our Exchange virtual server, to the new distributed port group.

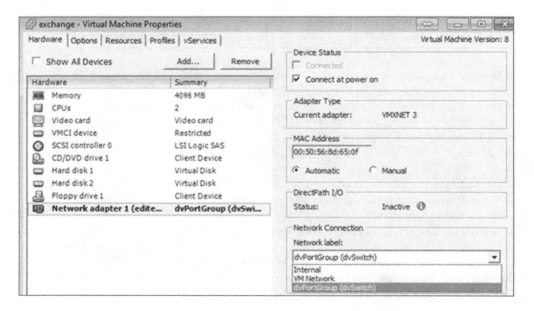

After editing the virtual machine settings, and selecting network adapter 1, notice that the Network Connection drop-down options include the new distributed port group named dvPortGroup. Select that option to move the virtual machine. The move should be very quick. We have moved running virtual machines and seen only one network packet drop.

And there you have it. We enabled NIOC on our distributed switch, created a new network resource pool, connected the distributed resource pool to our distributed port group, and modified our virtual machine to use the distributed port group. We are now routing virtual machine traffic from the Exchange server to the distributed port group.

Summary

This chapter started with differentiating physical and virtual networking. We introduced physical switches and their attributes. Next, we covered standard virtual switches and what they can offer. And we talked about specific advantages of having switches virtualized.

We presented the VMware switching technologies, including standard virtual switches and distributed virtual switches, sometimes called vNetwork Distributed Switch (vDS). Distributed virtual switches provide all the benefits of standard switches and a lot more.

Next, we talked about how to identify VMware virtual switch components, made up of virtual ports, port groups, and uplinks. We covered some of the attributes of the components, and what makes up a distributed virtual switch.

We discussed specific virtual switch policies and how you can leverage these policies to configure your VMware environment any way that you need to. We covered specific security settings, including promiscuous mode, forged transmits, and how to handle MAC address changes, traffic shaping, and failover and load balancing.

Finally, we talked about NIOC and how to leverage it to gain control over network traffic in your environment. You learned how to configure NIOC and how to manually assign a virtual machine to a NIOC–enabled distributed port group.

Exam Essentials

Be able to identify physical and virtual networking.   Both physical and virtual networking use ports, track MAC addresses, and provide layer 2 switching. Virtual networking, however, exists totally in software.

Be able to identify virtual switch features.   Virtual switches have an expandable number of ports, require port groups to route network traffic, route VMkernel traffic for management and other features, and can include uplink ports.

Be able to differentiate VMware virtual switch technologies.   The biggest differences between standard virtual switches and distributed virtual switches are that standard virtual switches can be created without a vCenter server, and port naming must be consistent for vMotion to work. Distributed virtual switches, on the other hand, are created at the data center level, require more-expensive licenses, and you no longer have to configure each ESXi host.

Know available features of distributed virtual switches.   Some advanced functionality of distributed virtual switches include the Network Health Check, bidirectional traffic filtering, link aggregation, private VLANs, Network vMotion, and third-party virtual switch support.

Know the virtual switch components.   It is important to know what makes up virtual switches. Virtual switches can have virtual ports for connecting virtual machines, port groups as a way to group and define the type of traffic, and uplinks that are used to route network traffic to physical networks.

Know the port group policies available on distributed switches.   It is important to know what policies are available. Port policies on distributed switches include resource allocation, monitoring, traffic filtering, private VLANs, and miscellaneous policies that can block all ports on a distributed port group.

Know the details of Network I/O Control (NIOC).   Four important functions are available by leveraging NIOC. These include isolation, limits, shares, and teaming.

Review Questions

You can find the answers in Appendix A.

1. Which of these features of a switch would identify it as a virtual switch?
   A. Tracks MAC addresses
   B. Routes layer 2 network traffic
   C. Has a lot of ports for server traffic
   D. Routes communication for VMkernel traffic through a port group

2. How does a switch keep track of traffic going through it?
   A. IP address
   B. MAC address
   C. Port number
   D. Time stamping

3. A virtual machine hosted by a virtual switch tries to send a network packet to a MAC address that the virtual switch does not recognize. What does the virtual switch do?
   A. Sends discovery packets on all virtual ports
   B. Keeps the route of the packet internal
   C. Virtual switch discards the packet
   D. Packet is handed off to the physical switch connected to the uplink

4. When do you choose what a port group will be used for?
   A. Creation time
   B. First use
   C. Dynamically
   D. When connected to a virtual machine

5. What is one thing for which you cannot use a port group configured for VMkernel traffic?
   A. vMotion
   B. NFS
   C. iSCSI
   D. Virtual machine traffic

6. A client workstation is trying to communicate over the network to a server connected to a different switch. The client workstation connected to a physical switch looks up the MAC address of the server and cannot find it. What does the switch do in order to route to the server?

    A. The switch will forward the packet to the core router.

    B. The switch will drop the packet.

    C. The switch will send the packet to all ports it has, except for the port connected to the client workstation.

    D. The switch will send the packet to all ports.

7. You have a brand new ESXi host along with a new storage solution that leverages iSCSI. You dedicate a network port for the storage and you create a new port group for the storage. What kind of connection type can you choose?

    A. Virtual machine traffic.

    B. VMkernel.

    C. Virtual machine or VMkernel traffic.

    D. You cannot use networking to connect to iSCSI.

8. Which one of these does not apply to both physical and virtual switches?

    A. Route network traffic

    B. Expandable number of ports

    C. Know about MAC addresses

    D. Required to communicate

9. What is the minimum required to route network traffic between 20 virtual machines evenly spread across three ESXi servers?

    A. One standard virtual switch

    B. One standard and one distributed switch

    C. Three standard switches

    D. Two standard virtual switches and one distributed switch

10. You are in charge of a business network with eight ESXi hosts in a cluster. You have a standard virtual switch on each host that you use for routing virtual machine traffic. You really want to make it easier to configure networking properties on each one of the ESXi hosts. You decide to create a distributed virtual switch. What level of license do you need?

    A. VMware Essentials license

    B. VMware Essentials Plus license

    C. VMware Enterprise license

    D. VMware Enterprise Plus license

11. You roll out a shiny new distributed virtual switch for your VMware environment, but you would like to filter traffic coming in and going out of your virtual machines. What is your best option?

   A. You could configure distributed switches to filter incoming as well as outgoing network traffic.

   B. You would have to create at least one more distributed switch.

   C. You would need a hardware appliance.

   D. You would have to configure a standard switch as a relay.

12. A distributed virtual switch can automatically check network settings for problems at regular intervals. What is this feature called?

   A. Network Health Check

   B. VLAN checking

   C. Link aggregation

   D. Network vMotion

13. What is link aggregation?

   A. Linking distributed virtual switches

   B. Consecutive virtual port naming

   C. Linking virtual switches together

   D. Combining the bandwidth of network cards

14. You start a new job to support an existing VMware environment. You notice that port mirroring is configured. What is port mirroring?

   A. A fault-tolerant way to clone a virtual machine

   B. A way to sync two virtual machines without a port group

   C. A tool for network administrators to troubleshoot virtual machine networks

   D. Mirroring one vCenter server to another vCenter server

15. What kind of objects can you create under a distributed virtual switch?

   A. Distributed virtual ports

   B. Distributed virtual uplinks

   C. Distributed virtual port groups and distributed virtual uplinks

   D. Distributed virtual port groups and standard switches

16. What is the best definition of a port group?

   A. A port group is used to connect the virtual switch to the physical network.

   B. A port group is like a physical switch but virtual. This is where virtual machines "plug in" their network connections.

   C. A port group is used to route traffic between physical servers.

   D. A port group is used to link vCenter servers.

17. What kind of network packets do virtual switches route?

   A. Standard networking packets

   B. Standard virtual switch proprietary packets

   C. Distributed virtual switch proprietary packets

   D. Proprietary packets from both standard and distributed virtual switches

18. What layer of network switching does a virtual switch operate on?

   A. Layer 1

   B. Layer 1 and 2

   C. Layer 3

   D. Layer 2

19. You are the engineer for a new VMware environment. You just added 200 virtual machines to a virtual switch that had only a few virtual machines connected to it before. What do you have to do in order to support this many virtual machines on the port group?

   A. Manually increase the number of ports on the port group.

   B. Move the virtual machines to a distributed port group.

   C. Nothing.

   D. Modify each virtual machine's network configuration.

20. You decide to create a distributed virtual switch. What must already exist there?

   A. ESXi

   B. vCenter Server

   C. A standard switch

   D. A physical switch

Chapter

6

Business Challenges Meet VMware Solutions

THE VCA-DCV TOPICS COVERED IN THIS CHAPTER INCLUDE THE FOLLOWING:

✓ **Apply VMware data center virtualization solutions to common business challenges**

- Apply VMware data center virtualization technologies to resolve common availability challenges

- Apply VMware data center virtualization technologies to resolve common management challenges

- Apply VMware data center virtualization technologies to resolve common optimization challenges

- Apply VMware data center virtualization technologies to resolve common scalability challenges

- Differentiate SMB and enterprise challenges and solutions

This chapter serves as a review of what you've learned in earlier chapters and connects real-world issues with the VMware solutions that can help resolve them. The chapter starts by discussing availability challenges, followed by management challenges, then optimization challenges, and finally scalability challenges. By delving into real-world scenarios, you will learn to identify the primary issues causing these challenges. You will also see which VMware product or solution can be used to resolve these root issues. The chapter ends by discussing the differences between small and midsize business (SMB) environments and larger enterprise environments. By the end of this chapter, you will be able to identify the root issue for common business challenges and recommend a VMware product or technology as a solution.

Availability Challenges and Solutions

As we discussed in Chapter 2, "VMware Solutions," *availability challenges* consist of anything that can cause an important application to become unavailable to the users who rely on it or that can cause an application outage to go on longer than absolutely necessary. This section presents availability challenges that businesses face as they continue to develop their corporate infrastructures. By evaluating real-world scenarios, you will see how a particular VMware solution can help resolve the primary issue and help produce a more reliable virtual environment.

This section presents real-world scenarios for the following VMware availability products and technologies:

- vMotion
- Storage vMotion
- Virtual machine snapshots
- High availability
- Fault tolerance
- vSphere Replication
- vSphere Data Protection
- Site Recovery Manager

By the end of this section, you will have a better understanding of the types of availability issues that larger companies experience and will be better prepared to recommend a VMware solution to help resolve them.

vMotion

This section presents two real-world scenarios in which vMotion can be used to mitigate an availability challenge.

Scenario A   Jennifer is a new system administrator for ABC Corp., a large manufacturing company that has approximately 120 ESXi hosts. One of Jennifer's first assignments is to plan out and perform a memory upgrade on eight of ABC Corp.'s production ESXi hosts. These upgrades must be completed quickly and without any downtime for any of the production virtual machines running on the ESXi hosts. Jennifer is not sure how to take down the ESXi hosts to upgrade them without also taking down the guests running on them. Which VMware technology can help Jennifer complete the upgrades?

> **Primary Issue**   ESXi hosts must be taken down to perform an upgrade without affecting the guests running on them.
>
> **Solution: vMotion**   Jennifer can use vMotion to move the running virtual machines off the ESXi host that she is planning to upgrade. Once all of the guests have been moved off the ESXi host and it has been placed into maintenance mode, it can be shut down and the memory upgrade can be performed. That host can then be brought back online, and Jennifer can move on to the next ESXi host, repeating the process until all the hosts have been upgraded.

Scenario B   Frank is a system administrator at XYZ Corp., a medium-sized technology company with a well-developed virtualization infrastructure. Frank has been receiving calls that several production virtual machines have been performing poorly lately. After researching the virtual machines, he determines that they are all on the same ESXi host and that at peak usage they are requesting more CPU and memory resources than the cluster has available. Which VMware technology can Frank use to resolve the peak usage issues?

> **Primary Issue**   The production virtual machines on an ESXi host require more CPU and memory resources than the host has available for them.
>
> **Solution: vMotion**   Frank can use vMotion to move some of the virtual machines to ESXi hosts that have available resources. By moving some virtual machines off the original ESXi host, more resources will be available for the virtual machines that were not moved, and performance should improve on all the virtual machines. By using vMotion, Frank can solve the performance issues without requiring downtime on any production virtual machines.

Storage vMotion

In this section's real-world scenario, Storage vMotion (svMotion) can be used to mitigate an availability challenge.

Scenario   Jill is a virtualization engineer at ABC Corp. She has been tasked with decommissioning some older 1 TB LUNs from her ESXi hosts and replacing them with newer 2 TB LUNs. ABC Corp. has recently experienced system outages that have left users unhappy, so performing these LUN upgrades without any interruption to the production virtual servers that reside on them is critical. How can Jill migrate the virtual machines from the existing 1 TB LUNs to newer 2 TB LUNs without taking an outage on the running production virtual servers?

Primary Issue   Virtual servers need to be migrated from existing LUNs to the new LUNs without any downtime.

Solution: Storage vMotion   Once Jill has added the new LUNs to the ESXi hosts, she can use svMotion to migrate the running virtual machines from their current 1 TB LUNs to the newer 2 TB LUNs. Once all the virtual machines have been moved off the 1 TB LUNs, she can remove them from her ESXi hosts. By using svMotion, Jill is able to migrate all her virtual machines to new storage without incurring any downtime or interruption to the applications running on them.

Virtual Machine Snapshots

This section presents a real-world scenario in which virtual machine snapshots can be used to mitigate an availability challenge.

Scenario   Bill is a server administrator at a large service integration company. In the next three months, Bill is planning to upgrade a custom application on several hundred of his virtual servers. The upgrade is fairly complicated, and in previous upgrades a small number of virtual servers were improperly configured and became unstable after the upgrade. These servers had to be rebuilt, causing a significant outage for some of Bill's clients. Which VMware technology can Bill use to reduce the recovery time for any virtual servers that become unstable after the latest upgrade is performed?

Primary Issue   Virtual servers require an upgrade and may need to have the upgrade rolled back if there are issues when the upgrade is done.

Solution: Virtual Machine Snapshots   Bill can use virtual machine snapshots to greatly reduce the recovery time of any virtual server that experiences issues after the upgrade. Bill can basically take a snapshot of the virtual server before he begins the upgrade process for each virtual server. Once the upgrade is complete, he can then monitor the virtual server for a while to see whether it is experiencing issues. If it is not experiencing issues, the snapshot can be deleted. If the virtual server does experience issues, Bill can quickly return it to the state it was in before the upgrade by reverting to the snapshot. Remembering to take a snapshot before an upgrade or patching isn't difficult, and it can make you look like a hero if things go bad and you are able to quickly fix them.

WARNING   Virtual machine snapshots can be extremely valuable when performing upgrades or patching on virtual machines, but they can also consume a large amount of space on your datastores. Be sure to delete snapshots after your virtual machine patching or upgrades are complete and have been validated. Also be careful about who you allow to create virtual machine snapshots. If too many people can create snapshots, you can quickly find yourself with storage issues.

High Availability

In the following real-world scenario, high availability (HA) can be used to mitigate an availability challenge.

Scenario John is a virtualization engineer at Virtual Corp., a large technology company with a well-established virtual infrastructure. John's new manager is not very familiar with virtual environments. During a staff meeting, the manager raises a concern that a hardware failure on a production ESXi host could cause many virtual machines to be down until someone is able to bring the ESXi host back up. He is particularly worried that if this occurred in the evening, the virtual machines could be down for a long period before the on-call engineer could get to the data center and bring the ESXi host back online. Which VMware technology should John review with his new manager to help him be more comfortable with the virtual environment?

> **Primary Issue** A hardware failure on an ESXi host could cause many virtual machines to be down for an extended period.

> **Solution: High Availability** John should discuss VMware high availability with his new manager. It has been in place at Virtual Corp. since the company began using virtual machines. John could explain that in the event of an ESXi host failure, HA will automatically restart the virtual machines that were running on the failed ESXi host on other ESXi hosts. The virtual machines experience a small amount of downtime as they are restarted on the new ESXi hosts, but that time is very short when compared to waiting for someone to manually move the virtual machines or manually restarting the ESXi host.

Fault Tolerance

This section presents a real-world scenario in which fault tolerance (FT) can be used to mitigate an availability challenge.

Scenario Mary is a Windows server administrator at XYZ Corp. She is somewhat familiar with virtual environments and understands that if an ESXi host with her virtual Windows servers running on it fails, the servers will be restarted on a different ESXi host with only a little downtime. She is concerned, though, that a few of her Windows servers are customer facing and business critical. These servers must have nearly no downtime, and the time it would take HA to restart them if the ESXi host failed would be too long. Which VMware technology can she use to make sure her critical virtual machines have extremely low unscheduled downtime due to a failure of the ESXi host?

> **Primary Issue** Certain critical virtual machines must have extremely low unscheduled downtime.

> **Solution: Fault Tolerance** Mary should ask the virtualization engineers at her company if they can implement FT for her critical virtual machines. FT allows a mirror to be created of a running virtual machine. As changes are made to the original virtual machine, they are also made to the mirror. If the original virtual machine fails, the mirror takes over without any application downtime.

WARNING   Fault tolerance is an incredible technology that can provide nearly zero unscheduled downtime for virtual machines, but it does have some limitations. The most glaring of these limitations is that the virtual machine using fault tolerance must have only a single CPU. This limitation rules out using fault tolerance on many critical production servers. Hopefully, this requirement will be eliminated in future releases of vSphere.

vSphere Replication

This section's real-world scenario uses vSphere Replication to mitigate an availability challenge.

Scenario   Dante is a server administrator at AtoZ Corp., a large utility company that has one data center in California and a second data center in Iowa. In a previous position with another company, Dante experienced a disaster that destroyed the company's data center. The data center was recovered, but the data that had changed on his servers from the time of the nightly backups until the time of the disaster was lost. You are the company virtualization engineer, and Dante has asked whether there is a way to leverage the virtual environment and the remote data center in Iowa to keep real-time backups of his critical virtual machines in California. Which VMware technology can you recommend to protect Dante's virtual machines?

Primary Issue   Critical virtual machines must be protected from data loss during a disaster.

Solution: vSphere Replication   vSphere Replication could be used to help meet Dante's requirements. This hardware-independent VMware technology allows running virtual machines to be replicated to another site to allow higher availability. The replication interval can be configured to reduce the amount of data that would be lost in a disaster. In the event that the primary site is down, the replicated virtual machines can be brought online at the backup site relatively quickly.

vSphere Data Protection

This section presents a real-world scenario in which vSphere Data Protection can be used to mitigate an availability challenge.

Scenario   Jack is the system administrator responsible for server backups at ABC Corp. ABC Corp. has been in the process of converting many of its physical servers into virtual machines. The company is using the same file-based backup process for virtual machines and physical servers. The process for restoring failed virtual machines is tedious and requires a new virtual machine to be created and then files from the old file-based backup to be restored to it. Jack asks you whether there may be a better way to back up the virtual machines so they could be restored more quickly and easily. What VMware solution can you recommend to simplify the process of virtual machine backups and restores?

Primary Issue   Virtual machines need to be easier to back up and restore.

Solution: vSphere Data Protection   You should consider recommending vSphere Data Protection, a VMware solution for backing up and restoring virtual machines. It can restore individual files to a virtual machine or restore an entire virtual machine much more quickly and easily than more-traditional file-backup methods. There are many backup solutions for virtual machines, but vSphere Data Protection is a good choice because it is made by VMware and is therefore tightly integrated into the VMware line of products.

Site Recovery Manager

In the following real-world scenario, Site Recovery Manager (SRM) can be used to mitigate an availability challenge.

Scenario   Michelle is the CIO of Rob Corp., a medium-sized technology company that is highly virtualized. Late last year, Rob Corp. ran a disaster-recovery drill that turned into a real disaster. Not only was the company unable to restore many of its virtual machines within required time limits, but a problem with network isolation caused a segment of its production virtual machines to go down during the disaster-recovery drill. To prevent anything like this from happening again, Michelle has instructed her virtualization engineers to come up with a better way of conducting disaster-recovery drills. She has required them to find a product that will allow disaster recoveries to be initiated quickly and that can be routinely tested (repeatedly) throughout the year without any chance of affecting their production network. Since this is a high-priority project, she has also reached out to your consulting firm for suggestions. Which VMware product would you recommend to meet all of Michelle's disaster-recovery requirements?

Primary Issue   Disaster recovery for virtual machines needs to be easier and more reliable.

Solution: Site Recovery Manager   Since you are an excellent consultant, you should recommend Site Recovery Manager. SRM is a VMware disaster-recovery solution that allows an entire data center to be restored by pressing a few buttons. It also allows disaster-recovery drills to be conducted at any time with complete network isolation so there is no chance of affecting the production servers during a drill.

WARNING   Site Recovery Manager is a powerful tool for performing disaster recoveries and drills, but it can also be dangerous if a recovery is accidentally or maliciously triggered. You should be careful about who has the ability to initiate a disaster recovery and who in the company has the authority to decide that a recovery should be initiated.

Now that you have seen several availability challenge scenarios and have a better understanding of the VMware products and technologies that can be used to help mitigate them, let's move on to the next type of challenge. In the next section, you will look at some real-world scenarios for management challenges and how to resolve them.

Management Challenges and Solutions

In Chapter 2, you learned that *management challenges* consist of issues that cause the environment to become harder to manage and understand. This section presents management challenges that are faced by companies every day as they attempt to keep control of their expanding virtual environments. By reviewing real-world scenarios, you will see how a given VMware solution can help resolve the primary issue and produce a more manageable environment.

This section covers the following VMware management products and technologies:

- Virtual machines/physical-to-virtual conversions
- vCenter Server
- vCenter Configuration Manager

Virtual Machines/Physical-to-Virtual Conversions

This section presents a real-world scenario in which virtual machines and physical-to-virtual (P2V) conversions can be used to mitigate a management challenge.

Scenario   Mario is the manager of the server team at Z-to-A Corp., a medium-sized technology company that is rapidly expanding. Mario tells you that one of his biggest management headaches is ensuring that any out-of-date or unsupported hardware is removed from the network. Many of his servers are running on older hardware that will need to be replaced or decommissioned. Since many of the newer servers being added to the environment are deployed as virtual machines, he would like to easily virtualize his older servers without having to completely reinstall everything that is on them. What VMware technology can Mario use to convert his physical servers to virtual machines?

Primary Issue   Older physical servers need to be converted to virtual servers.

Solution: Virtual Machines/P2V Conversions   Mario can convert his existing physical servers to virtual machines by using P2V conversions. P2V conversions allow existing physical servers to be converted into virtual machines without needing to reinstall any of the physical server's software. Using P2V conversions, many physical servers can quickly be converted into virtual machines. P2V conversions can be an ideal solution for replacing older physical servers that are running on end-of-life hardware with fully configured and easily upgradeable virtual machines.

vCenter Server

In this section's real-world scenario, vCenter Server can be used to mitigate a management challenge.

Scenario   Syed is the IT manager at a medium-sized production company. He would like to implement server virtualization so that his group and the company can start to benefit from the advantages of being virtualized. Syed's director has expressed reservations about moving into virtualization because he has heard that virtual environments can be difficult to manage. Which VMware technology should Syed discuss with his director to show that VMware takes management of the environment seriously and has tools that can provide centralized management?

Primary Issue   Concerns exist that management of a virtual environment can become too complicated.

Solution: vCenter Server   Syed should talk to his director about vCenter Server, a primary tool used to manage virtual environments. It provides a central point of management for administrators to perform most of the management tasks for the environment. Many of VMware's other products plug into vCenter Server and can be managed from within the vCenter console.

vCenter Configuration Manager

In this section, our real-world scenario uses vCenter Configuration Manager (VCM) to mitigate a management challenge.

Scenario   Kim is the IT director for BigBucks Corp., a large investment bank. Because it handles many government-backed home loans, it is heavily regulated by the FTC. Every three months, Kim must provide a certified report showing any configuration changes that have occurred in the environment and account for any systems that deviate from their established configurations. Developing this report is an extremely tedious process requiring a lot of employee man hours. The report is also complicated, so it is hard to be sure all the data is completely accurate. What VMware technology would you recommend to help Kim produce this report more efficiently and more accurately?

Primary Issue   Configuration changes in the environment must be tracked and reported.

Solution: vCenter Configuration Manager   VCM is a powerful VMware solution for tracking, reporting, and alerting on configuration changes in a virtual environment. It allows configuration baselines to be created for virtual servers and then tracks against those baselines any changes that are made. It can be used to quickly and accurately generate configuration change reports that can be certified and turned into regulators. Using VCM will free up resources in Kim's group to perform other tasks in the BigBucks virtual environment.

vCenter Configuration Manager is undergoing a name change to vRealize Configuration Manager in the newer releases of vSphere. On the exam it was referred to by the name vCenter Configuration Manager so I will use that name in this chapter, but in a future release of the exam the name is likely to change.

Next let's look at real-world scenarios and solutions for optimization challenges.

Optimization Challenges and Solutions

In Chapter 2, you learned that *optimization challenges* consist of anything that can cause applications to run at less-than-peak performance or can cause resources to be wasted. In this section, you will look at optimization challenges that many companies face as their environments grow. By reviewing real-world scenarios, you will see how a given VMware solution can help resolve the primary issue and produce a more efficient virtual environment.

This section covers the following VMware optimization products and technologies:

- vCenter Operations Manager
- Thin provisioning
- Distributed switches with QoS
- Distributed Power Management
- Storage I/O Control (SIOC)
- vFlash
- VM storage profiles
- Memory ballooning
- Transparent page sharing

vCenter Operations Manager

This section describes two real-world scenarios in which vCenter Operations Manager (vCOps) can be used to mitigate an optimization challenge.

Scenario A   Andre is the IT manager for a large technology company that has several thousand virtual machines. Andre would like to make sure his environment is running optimally and discover any resource bottlenecks that can be causing it to operate at less-than-peak performance. Which VMware technology could Andre use to monitor his virtual environment and identify any opportunities to have it run better?

> **Primary Issue**   Identify performance bottlenecks in a virtual environment that can be causing it to perform less than optimally.

> **Solution: vCenter Operations Manager**   Andre could use vCOps to help discover any performance bottlenecks in his virtual environment. vCOps continuously collects metrics from the virtual environment and uses them to determine where a performance bottleneck is occurring.

Scenario B   Andre would also like to determine whether any of his virtual machines have been assigned resources that they are not using. He wants to right-size his virtual machines so they have the resources they need but do not have additional resources that are wasted.

> **Primary Issue**   Identify wasted resources on virtual machines.

Solution: vCenter Operations Manager   Andre could use vCenter Operations Manager to identify wasted resources as well. By keeping metrics on the virtual machines over time, vCOps can determine the amount of CPU and memory used and compare that to the resources assigned. vCOps can generate reports that show each virtual machine, how much CPU and memory it is assigned, and how much CPU and memory it actually uses. This report can then be used to right-size the virtual machines.

Identifying virtual machines that have been overprovisioned with CPUs can be important to the performance of your virtual machines. Giving a virtual machine too many CPUs not only keeps you from being able to use those CPU resources elsewhere, but also, in many cases, causes the virtual machine to run poorly. Because of the way virtual machines share physical CPUs on the ESXi hosts, virtual machines with more CPUs assigned to them than they need can experience high CPU wait times and poor performance. It is counterintuitive but often true.

Thin Provisioning

In the following real-world scenario, thin provisioning can be used to mitigate an optimization challenge.

Scenario   Melanie is a server administrator at XYZ Corp. She has noticed that many of the company's deployed virtual machines use only a small fraction of the drive space configured for them. She would like to reclaim some of this drive space to reduce the need to buy additional storage. She also would like to be more efficient when drive space is assigned to new virtual machines. Which VMware technology could Melanie use to reclaim the wasted disk space and keep this situation from happening again as new virtual machines are deployed?

Primary Issue   Wasted disk space needs to be reclaimed from virtual machines.

Solution: Thin Provisioning   Melanie could use thin provisioning to reclaim the wasted disk space from the existing virtual machines and when deploying new virtual machines. Thin provisioning is a VMware technology that allows virtual machines to conserve disk space by consuming only the amount of space they actually need and by expanding as more space is needed. Existing virtual machines can have their disks converted to thin provisioning by using Storage vMotion and selecting Thin Provision for the drives.

Thin provisioning your virtual machines can greatly increase the number of virtual machines that can fit on a datastore, but it comes with some risk. If you are not careful and the thin-provisioned virtual machines attempt to use more space than is available in the datastore, various issues can arise. These issues can range from one of the virtual machines freezing to all of the virtual machines on the datastore freezing. You must periodically check your datastores to make sure that sufficient space is available for your thin-provisioned virtual machines to grow.

Distributed Switches with QoS

In this section, our real-world scenario uses distributed switches with QoS to mitigate an optimization challenge.

Scenario   Martin is a server administrator at Planes Corp. Planes Corp. is a large provider of administrative support to the aviation industry and has a well-developed virtualization environment. Martin has servers that are considered critical to Planes Corp.'s ability to support its customers and he has asked whether there is a way to give these servers greater access to the network than the other virtual servers on the same ESXi host. Which VMware technology could you suggest that would allow Martin to give certain virtual servers greater access to the network than others?

Primary Issue   Certain virtual servers need priority access to the network.

Solution: Distributed Switches with QoS   Martin could use distributed switches with QoS to give the machines the network access they need. Distributed Switch with QoS is a VMware technology that allows the network traffic of certain virtual machines to be prioritized over other virtual machines on the same ESXi host to make sure they are running optimally.

When associated with a distributed switch, *QoS* stands for *quality of service*. QoS is the idea that certain metrics such as transmission rates and error rates can be improved and, to a limited degree, guaranteed to certain ports on the switch. QoS can be useful for virtual machines that are running applications dependent on continuous transmission over the network, such as streaming video.

Distributed Power Management

This section presents a real-world scenario in which Distributed Power Management (DPM) can be used to mitigate an optimization challenge.

Scenario   Melissa is the CIO of Qwerty Co., a large keyboard manufacturer. Qwerty Co. is trying to implement new programs to become a more "green" company and reduce its energy usage. Melissa is happy with the power savings the company has achieved by virtualizing many of its older, inefficient physical servers, but she is hoping to leverage the virtualized environment to further reduce energy usage. Which VMware technology should Melissa look into to help reduce energy costs?

Primary Issue   Electrical usage needs to be reduced.

Solution: Distributed Power Management   Melissa should look into Distributed Power Management. DPM allows companies to save on electrical costs. It uses vMotion and wake-on-LAN technologies to save energy by powering off ESXi hosts when virtual machine demand is low and powering them back on as the virtual machine demand increases.

Storage I/O Control

In the following real-world scenario, Storage I/O Control (SIOC) can be used to mitigate an optimization challenge.

Scenario Mike is a server administrator at ABC Corp. He tells you that a few database servers that are critical to the company are having trouble competing against other virtual machines for access to storage. He asks whether there is any way to give these virtual machines priority access to the storage. Which VMware technology would you recommend to help resolve Mike's storage access issue?

Primary Issue Certain servers need priority access to storage resources.

Solution: Storage I/O Control Mike could use SIOC. SIOC allows the storage traffic of certain virtual machines to be prioritized to make sure they are running optimally.

vFlash

This section's real-world scenario uses vFlash to mitigate an optimization challenge.

Scenario Rick is a server administrator for a branch office of a large insurance company. The branch office has one ESXi host, and Rick has recently noticed that the performance of the virtual machines running on it has been decreasing. After researching the issue, he has discovered that the virtual machines are experiencing memory swapping to disk due to a lack of available memory. The ESXi host is already configured with as much memory as it can hold, and there is no plan or budget to add a new ESXi host to the branch office for approximately eight months. Rick has asked whether anything can be done to reduce the impact of the memory swapping until the new ESXi host is deployed. Which VMware technology would you recommend to Rick?

Primary Issue Disk swapping is causing virtual machine performance to suffer.

Solution: vFlash Rick should explore the possibility of running vFlash on his ESXi host. vFlash is a VMware technology that allows virtual machines to use solid-state drives on the ESXi host as their cache to increase performance and reduce the impact of memory swapping. Rick would need to find enough money in the budget to purchase a solid-state drive to add to the ESXi host, but these can be purchased for under $200, and he would not need a large drive to implement vFlash.

VM Storage Profiles

This section describes a real-world scenario that uses VM storage profiles to mitigate an optimization challenge.

Scenario Chris is the CIO of a growing technology company that provides applications on demand to its clients. Recently a large high-performance disk array was installed in his data center. Since space on the new disk array is limited and expensive, Chris would like to make sure that only virtual machines that need the high performance are located on it. Which VMware technology could Chris use to make sure that virtual machines are running on the class of storage that they need?

Primary Issue   Virtual machine files need to be located on the required class of storage.

Solution: VM Storage Profiles   Chris could use VM storage profiles. VM storage profiles allow each virtual machine disk to be assigned to a class of storage. Once a storage profile is assigned to a drive, it will be allowed to run only on storage that meets the requirements of the profile.

Memory Ballooning

In the following real-world scenario, memory ballooning can be used to mitigate an optimization challenge.

Scenario   Phillip is a Windows server administrator at a large technology company. He is in charge of several high-profile virtual machines. He has heard that if the ESXi host that these virtual machines are on is running low on available memory, it has a mechanism to reclaim memory from some virtual machines and make it available to other virtual machines. He does not fully understand how this works and is concerned that his virtual machines could be negatively impacted if memory is taken from them. Which VMware technology should you explain to him to ease his concerns about memory?

Primary Issue   Memory being reclaimed from virtual machines could cause performance issues.

Solution: Memory Ballooning   You should explain memory ballooning to Philip. Memory ballooning is a VMware technology that allows unused memory that is being held by a virtual machine to be reclaimed and used by other virtual machines. It reclaims only unused memory and will not cause performance issues on the virtual machine from which it reclaims the memory.

VMware Tools

Memory ballooning can occur only on virtual machines that have the VMware Tools software package installed. VMware Tools is a collection of drivers that is optimized for virtual machines and should be installed on all the virtual machines in your environment. It includes not only the driver that allows memory ballooning but also optimized network drivers for various virtual machine operating systems.

Transparent Page Sharing

In this section's real-world scenario, transparent page sharing can be used to mitigate an optimization challenge.

Scenario   Jonathan is the manager of the server team at a medium-sized shipping company. At a recent conference, he was told that he can improve memory utilization by placing his Linux virtual machines on one ESXi host and his Windows servers on a different ESXi host. His team supports many Windows virtual machines, so he thinks he may be able to improve memory utilization even further by separating the virtual machines across his ESXi hosts by the version of Windows they are running. He doesn't exactly understand how this could work and has asked you to research it and make a recommendation. Which VMware technology would you recommend?

Primary Issue   Memory utilization needs to be maximized.

Solution: Transparent Page Sharing   Jonathan should look into transparent page sharing, which allows an ESXi host to better utilize its available memory by comparing the memory blocks of virtual machines and keeping any identical blocks in only one location. To maximize the memory advantage from transparent page sharing, the virtual machines running on the ESXi host should be as similar as possible so they will have more identical memory blocks. Virtual machines can be separated by operating system and by the software running on them to fully optimize transparent page sharing.

Next let's consider some real-world scenarios and solutions for scalability challenges.

Scalability Challenges and Solutions

In Chapter 2, you learned that *scalability challenges* consist of anything that can cause issues as a company's infrastructure continues to grow or that limits the company's ability to quickly meet new challenges. This section presents scalability challenges that many companies face as their environments expand and the demands to do more, faster, continue to increase. As you review these real-world scenarios, you will see how a given VMware solution can help resolve the primary issue and produce a more responsive virtual environment.

This section covers real-world scenarios for the following VMware scalability products and technologies:

- Virtual machines
- Virtual machine templates
- Distributed Resource Scheduler
- Storage DRS
- vSphere storage appliance
- Hot add
- Distributed virtual switches

Virtual Machines

This section presents a real-world scenario in which virtual machines can be used to mitigate a scalability challenge.

Scenario   Chris is a director for Big Corp., a rapidly expanding multinational corporation. Big Corp. plans to deploy more than 1,000 new servers in the next six months. Its current process for adding a new server is to order new hardware, wait for it to arrive, install the hardware in the data center, and then install the operating system on the hardware. Big Corp. has streamlined this process and can have a new physical server installed and configured in its data center within 19 days of ordering it. However, Chris is concerned that this process will not scale up to meet the company's demand for new servers. What VMware technology could you recommend to help Chris more efficiently deploy new servers?

Primary Issue   Many new servers need to be deployed in a relatively short time period.

Solution: Virtual Machines   Chris could use virtual machines to meet his growing demand for new servers. Once a virtual infrastructure is in place, new virtual machines can easily be deployed within hours instead of the weeks or months it generally takes to deploy new physical servers. Many larger companies have provisioning systems that can deploy new virtual machines in less than an hour.

When deploying a large number of new physical servers, some will inevitably arrive at your data center in nonworking condition. Some may get damaged in shipping and others may suffer from production errors. These broken physical servers can cause real issues for deployment timelines and must be taken into account when considering to use physical or virtual servers for your large deployments.

Virtual Machine Templates

In this section, our real-world scenario uses virtual machine templates to mitigate a scalability challenge.

Scenario   Clyde is a server administrator at XYZ Corp. He has been tasked to deploy 20 new web servers for a large rollout of a new web-based application. All of the web servers will be virtual machines and will have the same operating system and the same software installed on them. They will require some customization, but this will be done by the web development team after the servers are placed online. It will take Clyde several hours to install the operating systems and additional software on each new web server. He has asked whether you know of any way that he can speed up the process for rolling out these new web servers. Which VMware technology would you recommend to help Clyde more efficiently deploy the new virtual servers?

Primary Issue   Many similar virtual machines need to be deployed in a short time frame.

Solution: Virtual Machine Templates   Clyde could use virtual machine templates to help him dramatically reduce the amount of work he will need to perform to deploy the new web servers. Using templates will also help get the servers configured more quickly and with less chance of any configuration errors. Clyde would need to fully configure one of the new web servers. Then he could convert that configuration into a template and use that template to deploy the remaining web servers. Using virtual machine templates, Clyde could complete the deployment in a matter of hours instead of the week or more it would take him to deploy them from scratch.

Distributed Resource Scheduler

In the following real-world scenario, the Distributed Resource Scheduler (DRS) can be used to mitigate a scalability challenge.

Scenario   Michael is a new server engineer at Sprocket Co., a medium-sized manufacturing company that has a relatively new virtualization infrastructure. Michael is concerned that as new virtual machines are added to the ESXi hosts, they may not be distributed evenly across the hosts, leaving some of them heavily overused while others are sitting idle. He has asked whether there is some way to make sure that virtual machine workloads are evenly distributed across his ESXi hosts. Which VMware technology would you recommend to help Michael keep the demand on his ESXi hosts balanced?

> **Primary Issue**   Some ESXi hosts may be overburdened while others may be underutilized.
>
> **Solution: Distributed Resource Scheduler**   Michael could use the DRS to help spread the virtual machine workload across his ESXi hosts. The DRS allows virtual machine workloads to be automatically load-balanced across multiple ESXi hosts, to remove the problem of hot spots causing one ESXi host to be overwhelmed while others go underutilized.

Storage DRS

In this section's real-world scenario, Storage DRS can be used to mitigate a scalability challenge.

Scenario   Sarah is a virtualization engineer at Big Corp., a large technology firm that has a well-developed virtualization infrastructure. Sarah has recently been made aware that certain datastores are experiencing very high utilization during backups while other datastores appear to be barely used. She would like to have her datastore demand balanced across all available datastores. Which VMware technology should Sarah confirm is running on her clusters to automatically load balance datastore utilization across all of her datastores?

> **Primary Issue**   Some datastores are experiencing very high utilization, while others appear to be nearly unused.
>
> **Solution: Storage DRS**   Sarah should confirm that she has Storage DRS configured on her clusters. Storage DRS is a VMware technology that allows virtual machine files and demand to be load balanced across storage arrays to avoid hot spots, whereby one datastore or storage array is overwhelmed while others go underutilized.

vSphere Storage Appliance

This section describes a real-world scenario in which the vSphere Storage Appliance (VSA) can be used to mitigate a scalability challenge.

Scenario   Emily is a virtualization engineer for a large insurance company. The company has a primary data center in Atlanta and smaller branch offices located throughout the country. Emily would like to run the same virtualization technologies at her branch offices as she does at the primary data center, but many of them require the ESXi hosts to have shared storage. Adding new shared storage arrays at all branch offices would not be feasible. Emily has asked whether she could use local drives on the ESXi hosts at the branch office and still be able to use the applications that require shared storage. Which VMware technology would you recommend to resolve Emily's storage issue?

> **Primary Issue**   Virtualization technologies that require shared storage are needed at branch offices that do not have shared storage.

> **Solution: vSphere Storage Appliance**   Emily could implement the VSA at her branch offices. VSA is a VMware technology that can be used to aggregate unused disks on ESXi hosts and use them as shared storage. This can be effective for branch offices that do not have shared storage.

Hot Add

In the following real-world scenario, hot add can be used to mitigate a scalability challenge.

Scenario   Megan is a server engineer for a medium-sized retail company. She has been given the task of upgrading the memory on several production Windows 2008 R2 virtual servers to handle additional load. Because these are production servers, she will not be able to shut them down to perform the upgrades until after midnight. She would like to perform the upgrades earlier in the day and has asked whether there is any way that she could upgrade the memory on these servers without needing to shut them down. Which VMware technology would you recommend to help her with the memory upgrades?

> **Primary Issue**   Memory on a virtual machine needs to be upgraded without having to first shut down the machine.

> **Solution: Hot Add**   Hot add would allow Megan to upgrade the memory on the virtual machines without needing to shut them down first. Hot add is a VMware technology that allows CPUs or memory to be added to running virtual machines, allowing them to scale up to higher workloads without downtime.

Distributed Virtual Switches

This section presents a real-world scenario in which distributed virtual switches (dvSwitches) can be used to mitigate a scalability challenge.

Scenario   Casey is the manager of the server virtualization team at Envirotech Corp., a medium-sized technology company that is rapidly expanding. Casey has noticed that as large numbers of new ESXi hosts are deployed, mistakes are being made in the configuration of the virtual switches. It has also become more difficult to update the virtual switches as changes are made to the underlying network. She has asked whether there is a better way to configure virtual switches on the ESXi hosts that would allow them to be more consistent and easier to change when changes are required. Which VMware technology would you recommend Casey start using for her virtual switches?

Primary Issue   As more and more virtual switches are created, they are becoming harder to keep consistent and to update when the network changes.

Solution: Distributed Virtual Switches   Casey should look into dvSwitches. A distributed virtual switch is a type of virtual switch that can be deployed once and can be attached to newly created ESXi hosts.

It has the advantage of needing to be created only once and then it can be used on multiple ESXi hosts and allowing a single change point when changes are made to the network.

Now that you have had a chance to review the types of challenges that companies face and have seen them presented as real-world scenarios, let's take a step back and discuss the differences between the issues that are faced by small businesses versus those that are faced by large enterprise companies.

The Differences between SMB and Enterprise Challenges and Solutions

This section presents some of the differences between the challenges that are faced by small and medium-size businesses as compared to those faced by large enterprise environments. As you might have guessed, these differences are all related to size. A change that needs to be done to three or four ESXi hosts can be done manually but would be impractical to perform manually for 500 ESXi hosts and would need to be scripted. To reverse that, it would be impractical to write a script for a change that will be made only once or twice. The following VMware technologies would be used by larger companies to help simplify the management of their environments and may not provide significant advantages to smaller companies:

vSphere Replication   A smaller company may have only one location and would have nowhere to replicate a virtual machine to.

Site Recovery Manager   A smaller company may have only one location and may be able to use a more manual process for its disaster-recovery needs since it would have a smaller environment to recover.

vCenter Configuration Manager   Since a smaller company would have fewer machines to configure and monitor changes for, using a product like VCM may not be worth the expense.

Distributed Virtual Switches   Since a smaller company would have only a few ESXi hosts, the vSwitches on them could be configured and maintained without implementing dvSwitches.

vCenter Operations Manager   vCOps is designed to monitor large virtual environments and gather metrics on them. Other less-expensive tools could be used for a smaller environment.

VM Storage Profiles   It is likely that a smaller company will have only one class of shared storage, making VM storage profiles unnecessary.

Distributed Power Management   DPM is meant to help save larger companies money by reducing electrical costs. A smaller company may have only a few ESXi hosts, and the savings from shutting them down could be negligible.

Summary

In this chapter, we elaborated on the discussion from Chapter 2. We discussed the types of challenges faced by businesses and gave real-world examples of them. We then discussed the VMware technologies that can be used to help mitigate these challenges.

We started by giving real-world scenarios of availability challenges that medium and large companies face on a regular basis. These include the need to upgrade ESXi hosts without any downtime to the virtual machines and the need to be able to recover from failed software upgrades. Once we identified the primary issue from each scenario, we briefly looked at the VMware products and technologies that can be used to mitigate them: vMotion, Storage vMotion, virtual machine snapshots, high availability, fault tolerance, vSphere Replication, vSphere Data Protection, and Site Recovery Manager.

Next we looked at some scenarios for management challenges. These included the ability to remove older hardware from the data center and to centrally manage the virtual environment. Again we identified the primary issues presented in the scenarios and the VMware products and technologies that can be used to mitigate them: virtual machines/P2V conversions, vCenter Server, and vCenter Configuration Manager.

We then looked at scenarios for the optimization challenges that businesses face. These challenges include ensuring that the virtualization environment is not experiencing performance bottlenecks and maximizing the utilization of CPU and memory resources. We looked at the VMware technologies that can be used to help businesses achieve full optimization: vCenter Operations Manager, thin provisioning, distributed switches with QoS, Distributed Power Management, Storage I/O Control (SIOC), vFlash, memory ballooning, and transparent page sharing.

Finally, we moved on to look at the common scalability challenges that businesses face. We reviewed scenarios for these challenges that included the need to rapidly deploy new virtual machines and to deploy shared storage solutions to branch offices. Once we identified the primary issue from each scenario, we briefly looked at the VMware products and technologies that can be used to mitigate them: virtual machines, virtual machine templates, Distributed Resource Scheduler, Storage DRS, vSphere Storage Appliance, hot add, and distributed virtual switches.

We finished the chapter by briefly looking at some of the differences between SMBs and enterprise businesses. We listed some of the VMware technologies that can be helpful for larger businesses but may not provide the same level of benefits for smaller companies.

Exam Essentials

Know how to read a real-world business scenario and be able to identify the availability challenges that are presented in the scenario. Remember from Chapter 2 that availability challenges consist of anything that can cause an important application to become unavailable to the users who rely on it or that can cause an outage to go on longer than absolutely necessary.

Be able to recommend a VMware technology that can be used to mitigate an availability challenge after it has been identified. The following technologies can be used to mitigate many availability challenges, and you will need a basic understanding of them for the exam: vMotion, Storage vMotion, virtual machine snapshots, high availability, fault tolerance, vSphere Replication, vSphere Data Protection, and Site Recovery Manager.

Know how to read a real-world business scenario and be able to identify the management challenges that are presented in the scenario. Remember from Chapter 2 that management challenges consist of issues that cause the environment to become harder to manage and understand.

Be able to recommend a VMware technology that can be used to mitigate a management challenge after it has been identified. The following technologies can be used to mitigate many management challenges, and you will need a basic understanding of them for the exam: virtual machines, vCenter Server, and vCenter Configuration Manager.

Know how to read a real-world business scenario and be able to identify the scalability challenges that are presented in the scenario. Remember from Chapter 2 that scalability challenges consist of anything that can cause issues as a company's infrastructure continues to grow or that limits the company's ability to quickly meet new challenges.

Be able to recommend a VMware technology that can be used to mitigate a scalability challenge after it has been identified. The following technologies can be used to mitigate many scalability challenges, and you will need a basic understanding of them for the exam: virtual machines, virtual machine templates, Distributed Resource Scheduler, Storage DRS, the vSphere Storage Appliance, hot add, and distributed virtual switches.

Know how to read a real-world business scenario and be able to identify the optimization challenges that are presented in the scenario. Remember from Chapter 2 that optimization challenges consist of anything that can cause applications to run at less-than-peak performance or can cause resources to be wasted.

Be able to recommend a VMware technology that can be used to mitigate an optimization challenge after it has been identified. The following technologies can be used to mitigate many optimization challenges, and you will need a basic understanding of them for the exam: vCenter Operations Manager, thin provisioning, VM storage profiles, Distributed Switch with QoS, Distributed Power Management, Storage I/O Control, vFlash, memory ballooning, and transparent page sharing.

Review Questions

You can find the answers in Appendix A.

1. Connie is an IT manger from XYZ Corp. She tells you that she has a critical virtual machine that must not have any unscheduled downtime. Which of the following VMware technologies would you recommend she implement to ensure the uptime of the virtual machine?

   A. Fault tolerance

   B. High availability

   C. vSphere Data Protection

   D. vSphere Replication

2. Frank is a new member of the virtualization team at XYZ Corp. He has been tasked with upgrading the memory on their VMware ESXi hosts. Since he is new to virtualization, he doesn't understand how he can take the host servers down to upgrade the memory without shutting down the guests that are running on them. Which of the following VMware technologies would you explain to Frank to help him perform the memory upgrade?

   A. Storage DRS

   B. Hot add

   C. Storage vMotion

   D. vMotion

3. To save money on new hardware, the administrators at XYZ Corp. have placed multiple production applications on each physical server. In the beginning this seemed like a good idea, but they have started to experience increased downtime in some of their primary applications due to incompatibilities between the applications running on a single server. They have also encountered times when an upgrade of one application required a server outage, causing all of the applications on the physical server to be down. Which VMware technology would you recommend to help them with application isolation?

   A. Fault tolerance

   B. Templates

   C. vCenter

   D. Virtual machines

4. The vSphere Storage Appliance could be used to help resolve which of the following real-world business challenges?

   A. ABC Corp. wants to extend its enterprise solutions to its branch offices but does not want to purchase shared disks for each branch office.

   B. ABC Corp. wants to be able to load balance virtual machines across storage arrays to avoid hot spots, whereby one storage array is overused and others go underused.

   C. ABC Corp. wants to be able to load balance virtual machines across ESXi hosts to remove the problem of hot spots, whereby one ESXi host is overused while other go underused.

   D. ABC Corp. wants to configure virtual machines to take up only the amount of disk space they are actually using.

5. Which of the following business scenarios would be the best fit for the VMware technology Distributed Power Management?

   A. A company that has a consistent demand for virtual machines 24 hours a day.

   B. A company that has a large demand for virtual servers during the day and less of a demand in the evening.

   C. A company whose demand for virtual machines rises and falls often throughout a 24-hour period.

   D. None of these would be a good fit for Distributed Power Management.

6. Fast Corp. is a rapidly growing company that expects to deploy several hundred Windows virtual machines in the next year. Company officials are concerned that their current process of manually creating new virtual machines and then installing operating systems and their custom software on them will not be efficient enough to meet their expansion goals. Which VMware technology would you advise them to use to deploy their new virtual machines more efficiently?

   A. Hot add

   B. Templates

   C. Thin provisioning

   D. vFlash

7. Jane is a systems engineer at a large industrial company. She is concerned that new virtual machines that are incorrectly configured could cause issues for the current production virtual machines on the ESXi hosts that they are deployed to. To avoid this issue, she would like to have all new virtual machines deployed to a single ESXi host. Then, after they have been fully tested, they would be moved to a different ESXi host with other production virtual machines. She would like to manually perform the move of each virtual machine so she can be sure it has been fully tested. Which of the following VMware technologies can she use to perform the move of the virtual machine?

   A. Distributed Resource Scheduler

   B. Hot add

   C. Storage DRS

   D. vMotion

8. James is an IS director for a corporation that has many virtualized servers. His company is heavily regulated by the government, so he must be able to accurately track changes to the virtual machines and alert on any deviations from company standards. Which of the following VMware technologies would you recommend to James?

   A. Distributed Resource Scheduler

   B. vCenter Server

   C. vCenter Configuration Manager

   D. vSphere Data Protection

9. Muhammad is a new system administrator for a medium-sized electrical utility. He is considering virtualizing many of his servers but is concerned that if a physical host server crashes, all of the guest servers running on it would be down until the physical host could be brought back up. Which VMware technology should you recommend to ensure that his virtual servers would be down for only a short time?

   A. Fault tolerance

   B. High availability

   C. vSphere Data Protection

   D. vSphere Replication

10. John is an administrator at ABC Corp. He mentions that he has an application server that must have priority access to the network as compared to other virtual machines that are on the same host. Which VMware technology would you recommend to him?

   A. Distributed Switch with QoS

   B. Storage DRS (SDRS)

   C. Storage I/O (SIOC)

   D. Thin provisioning

11. Sharee, a server administrator at XYZ Corp., has heard that the memory of an ESXi host can be overallocated to the virtual machines running on it. She has also heard that if the memory demand on the overallocated ESXi host is high, it may take memory from her Windows virtual machines. She is concerned that they may suffer performance issues. Which of the following VMware technologies should you discuss with Sharee to help assure her that her virtual machines will not suffer?

   A. Distributed Resource Scheduler

   B. Memory ballooning

   C. Transparent page sharing

   D. vFlash

12. Upper management at BIG Corp. is concerned that as new virtual machines are being deployed into the virtual environment, they are not being placed correctly onto ESXi hosts. They are worried that some of the ESXi hosts will become greatly overstressed while other ESXi hosts are being underutilized. Which of the following VMware technologies would you recommend to ensure that virtual machines will be evenly distributed across the ESXi hosts?

   A. Distributed Power Management

   B. Distributed Resource Scheduler

   C. High availability

   D. Site Recovery Manager

13. Syed is a virtualization engineer at ABC Corp. He has seen a report that the majority of his Windows virtual machines are using only a fraction of the drive space that has been assigned to them and he would like to reclaim the unused space and prevent this from happening again the future. Which of the following VMware technologies would you recommend to Syed to help him with his storage issues?

  A. Snapshots

  B. Thick provisioning

  C. Thin provisioning

  D. vFlash

14. Mark is the IT director for a growing company that is just starting to consider virtualizing its environment because company officials have heard they can save money in hardware and can make their environment more efficient. Mark's main concern is that a virtual environment can become complex, and he doesn't see any tool that can be used to manage the entire environment. Therefore, he is hesitant to move forward with any virtualization effort. Which of the following VMware tools should you discuss with Mark to help resolve his concerns?

  A. Distributed Resource Scheduler

  B. High availability

  C. Site Recovery Manager

  D. vCenter Server

15. Mike is a senior virtualization engineer at a large manufacturing company. He needs to decommission some smaller LUNs from his hosts and replace them with new, larger LUNs. His manager, who is not as experienced with virtualization, is concerned that the virtual machines located on those LUNs will need to be taken down to perform the decommissions. Which of the following VMware technologies should Mike explain to his manager to assure him that the decommissions can be performed without any downtime?

  A. Storage DRS

  B. Hot add

  C. Storage vMotion

  D. vMotion

16. Kim is a manager from ABC Corp. During a meeting to discuss virtualization, she explains that she has a few virtual machines that have continuously updating data that needs to be protected in the event of a disaster that could destroy their data center. Nightly backups are performed but are not sufficient to ensure that no data would be lost if there was a disaster during the day. Which VMware technology could she use to ensure that an up-to-date copy of her virtual machines could be brought online in the event of a disaster?

  A. Fault tolerance

  B. High availability

  C. vSphere Data Protection

  D. vSphere Replication

17. The Windows Server Support Team at a medium-sized company needs to upgrade their virtual servers to a new version of their production software. Team members are concerned that the upgrades could cause the servers to become unstable and that a long outage could occur if they needed to reinstall the servers and the older version of the software. Which VMware technology would you recommend to reduce their anxiety about the upgrade?

   A. High availability

   B. Hot add

   C. Snapshots

   D. vSphere Replication

18. Anna is an administrator at XYZ Corp. She tells you that XYZ has three database servers that must have priority access to company storage as compared to the other virtual machines that are also on the ESXi host. Which VMware technology would you recommend?

   A. Distributed switches

   B. Storage DRS (SDRS)

   C. Storage I/O Control (SIOC)

   D. Thin provisioning

19. Bill is an IT director at a large financial firm. Because the company handles financial accounts for external customers, it must have a thorough and easily testable disaster-recovery plan in place. Which VMware product would you recommend to allow Bill to have a comprehensive disaster-recovery plan that could be tested without interfering with daily operations?

   A. Fault tolerance

   B. High availability

   C. Site Recovery Manager

   D. vSphere Replication

20. Marcus is a virtualization engineer at ABC Corp, a large company with more than 1,000 virtual machines. Marcus has heard that he can get better memory utilization for his virtual machines by placing virtual machines that have the same operating systems on the same ESXi hosts, but he doesn't understand why. Which of the following VMware technologies should you discuss with Marcus?

   A. Distributed Resource Scheduler

   B. Memory ballooning

   C. Transparent page sharing

   D. vFlash

Appendices

Appendix
A

Answers to Review Questions

Chapter 1

1. D. All of these listed are advantages of data center virtualization. Fewer physical servers is the essence of consolidation. Of course, data center virtualization has many more advantages.

2. A. Data center virtualization converts physical hardware devices into software resources. This is a big deal and opens up flexibility, and in some cases, extreme cost savings. Data center virtualization is the virtual representation of a physical data center.

3. D. The number of virtual machines a hypervisor can host is always dependent on the physical resources available to the hypervisor and the amount of resources needed by the virtual machines.

4. C. The hypervisor separates the operating system and applications from the underlying physical hardware. The hypervisor plays the role of a resource traffic cop for all the virtual machines running on the host.

5. C. Consolidation is the key to cost saving and flexibility. Consolidation of physical servers to virtual servers means fewer physical servers. Fewer physical servers means less power is consumed and less cooling is required, which saves money. Of course, virtualization has a lot of advantages, but this is widely considered one of the biggest.

6. D. This is the key concept of isolation. A virtual machine being hosted on a physical server has no knowledge of other virtual machines on the same physical host. This provides a lot of benefits. This key concept addresses the old problem of one application taking down other applications on the same physical machine.

7. D. Distributed Power Management allows physical hosts to be powered down when not in use to save power costs.

8. B. The physical server in this scenario is called a *host*. When you have conversations, it is better to use a common vocabulary. This removes some of the confusion between a server running as a virtual machine and the physical server that runs the hypervisor.

9. D. VMware supports all of these devices and others as well. This makes a much smaller and more robust data center.

10. D. This is another example of OS/application isolation. Other virtual machines on this ESXi host know nothing about the failed Windows 2012 server.

11. A, B. Typically, you can save money on management costs as well as capital expenses as a direct result of data virtualization. Licenses are typically the same cost. However, you could argue that some vendors allow you to save money on licenses when operating systems are virtualized on the same host. But the details of licenses can change drastically from one day to the next, so here I take the conservative view and assume that A and B are the best choices.

12. D. *Consolidation* is a key term that you can expect on the exam. Remember that consolidation reduces the number of physical devices and therefore reduces power consumption and required cooling. It adds a lot of flexibility as well!

13. D. The main challenges addressed by virtualization are power usage, cooling, server cost, and virtual machine management costs. Once physical servers are virtualized, you can expect to start saving money on each of these.

14. A. The hypervisor is the physical ESXi host. The hypervisor is very small and often runs completely from flash RAM on the server hardware.

15. C. The definition of consolidation is reducing the number of physical devices (servers). This is one of the biggest goals of data center virtualization. Some companies make their data centers much smaller.

16. D. Only one of these is a benefit of data center virtualization. Virtualized environments make it much easier to deploy new servers. Servers can be deployed in minutes. Physical servers can take weeks.

17. D. All of these are physical hardware devices. Anything you can touch would be considered a physical device. Of course, all of these can be virtualized with VMware.

18. D. VMware ESXi host servers run the hypervisor. You use dedicated physical servers for these hosts running ESXi. However, the hypervisor is definitely the resource traffic cop.

19. A, B, C. A virtual machine consists of hardware, operating system, and applications, all virtualized. Strictly speaking, the virtual switch is not part of the virtual machine. The virtual switch exists within the ESXi host.

20. B. Providing virtual copies of server hardware to virtual machines is one of the biggest responsibilities of the hypervisor. The other is talking directly to the physical server hardware. Again, this is the resource traffic cop role. The virtual switches (answers C and D), which are not part of the virtual machine, provide switching of network packets. The vCenter server is the main management device used to coordinate other VMware solutions, like vMotion.

Chapter 2

1. A. A physical server failure is an availability challenge because the application that is running on that server would be unavailable to the users who rely on it. VMware high availability can be used to mitigate physical server failures.

2. B. Thin provisioning is a VMware technology that allows an administrator to assign a disk to a virtual machine of a maximum size, but the virtual machine will use only the space that it needs and will grow as additional space is needed until it reaches the maximum size that it has been allocated. Thin provisioning can greatly increase the number of virtual machines that can fit on a physical disk without affecting the performance of the virtual machines.

3. D. Storage I/O Control (SIOC) allows an administrator to assign a higher priority for access to storage for a given virtual machine or set of virtual machines.

4. A. Replacing outdated or unsupported hardware is a management challenge that can be accomplished by using physical-to-virtual conversions to replace physical servers with virtual machines.

5. C. Many administrators will place multiple applications on the same physical server to reduce the number of physical servers they require or because no additional physical servers are available. Because these servers share the same operating system, the failure of one application can cause the failure of the other applications on the server. When virtual machines are used, each application can reside on its own virtual machine, and the applications can be isolated from each other.

6. C. The need to rapidly add new servers is a scalability issue because it involves rapidly scaling up the virtual environment to handle new or expanding workloads. VMware templates enable an administrator to quickly deploy new virtual servers that are consistently configured.

7. C. Fault tolerance is a VMware solution for mitigating the failure of a single virtual machine. It allows two virtual machines to be connected so that if the first virtual machine fails, the other is ready to take over with no downtime. This can be extremely useful for applications that must have extremely high uptimes.

8. B. Snapshots allow an administrator to create a point-in-time restore point for a virtual machine. If a snapshot is taken before an application is patched or upgraded, and the application fails, it can be easily restored to the point where the snapshot was taken.

9. B. The hot-add capability allows resources including CPU and memory to be added to a running virtual machine without a reboot. The operating system of the virtual machine must be able to handle hot adds, so you are limited to using this on newer operating systems.

10. D. The vSphere Storage Appliance allows an administrator to aggregate the unused local drives on ESXi hosts and use them as shared storage. The VSA can allow large organizations to use the same technologies in branch offices that do not have shared storage as they do in their primary data centers and corporate offices.

11. B, D. Both the desire to reduce power usage whenever possible and the need to reclaim unused storage space are optimization issues. They both try to save resources and save money by not using more power than necessary and by reducing the amount of storage that needs to be purchased.

12. B. Storage vMotion can be used to move a virtual machine from its location on shared storage to another location on shared storage with no downtime for the virtual machine. This can be useful when maintenance needs to be performed on the storage or when older storage is being decommissioned.

13. B. VMware's vMotion technology allows an administrator to move a running virtual machine from one ESXi host to another with *no* downtime. vMotion can be extremely useful for moving all the virtual machines off an ESXi host when performing maintenance or hardware upgrades.

14. B. vSphere Data Protection is a backup solution from VMware that allows virtual machines to be easily backed up and restored. Using vSphere Data Protection, it is much easier to

restore a failed virtual machine than it is when using a more traditional file-based backup solution.

15. C. Once a virtual machine has been fully configured, it can be converted into a template. This template can then be used to deploy large numbers of new virtual machines that are very similar to the original virtual machine. Using templates can help increase the consistency of newly deployed virtual machines and therefore make them easier to manage.

16. C. High availability does not use vMotion to migrate virtual machines. HA moves virtual machines after the host they are running on has failed. vMotion moves virtual machines from one host to another host without an outage.

17. D. Storage DRS (SDRS) load balances virtual machines across different storage arrays by automatically moving virtual machines from one storage location to another. There is no downtime associated with the storage moves.

18. A. Distributed Power Management is a VMware technology that is designed to save electricity costs by powering off ESXi hosts when the computing demand is low and bringing them back up when the demand increases. It uses vMotion to move the virtual machines that are running on a host to another host before it powers it off.

19. A. Only fault tolerance allows a virtual machine to fail over without any downtime. It creates a mirror of the original machine, and any action that occurs on the original virtual machine also occurs on the mirror. If the original virtual machine fails, the mirror takes over with no downtime.

20. D. High availability actually restarts the virtual machine on a different host after the initial host has failed. It is important to remember that the virtual machines are restarted and will take a short outage if an HA event occurs.

Chapter 3

1. D. Site Recover Manager is your go-to guy here. Your CTO may not know how everything works, but as you explain what vCenter Site Recovery Manager does, you can do so in confidence. You can use Site Recovery Manager to test out your disaster-recovery plan during the work day!

2. B. The obvious answer here is to use vMotion to move the virtual machines to another host in an effort to free up the host with the failed power supply.

3. C. A hypervisor is the software layer installed on the physical hardware and it fulfills requests for resources by virtual machines.

4. D. A snapshot takes a point-in-time picture of a virtual machine. After creating a snapshot of a virtual machine, you should always be able to get back to the point in time the snapshot was taken.

5. A. vCenter Configuration Manager can be used to audit your VMware environment to make sure configuration settings are consistent.

6. C. Since these two departments must share a cluster, the best answer is to create resource pools for each. Limiting either department by the number of virtual machines or one ESX host will not guarantee splitting the resources. Creating a separate data center object for each department is impossible since a cluster cannot span data centers.

7. B. In fairness, a correct procedure for one company is not necessarily correct for others. However, you should assume a snapshot was taken before the Windows patch was installed. You probably wrote the procedure for installing patches yourself, right?

8. D. Fault tolerance is the only choice that has a chance to address the concerns. The other answers listed would be advantageous but would not address the specific concern here. Of course, you would have to talk him out of 100-percent uptime, which is unrealistic in any environment. For example, if a city-sized asteroid falls to Earth, your servers will likely no longer be running.

9. D. Compared to some other VMware solutions, NSX is fairly new for some. However, this product promises to shake up the networking industry. Anyone who suffered through network outages because of small firewall rule changes should be able to appreciate NSX. Leveraging NSX can simplify your network configuration. You would already have vCenter Server since it is required for distributed switches. vSphere Data Protection does a good job of backing up and restoring virtual machines but would not help here. And vCenter Operations arguably could help but is not the obvious choice that addresses the problem.

10. A. The best option here is Virtual SAN. By leveraging Virtual SAN, you can still have HA clusters, since Virtual SAN is shared. Local storage is not shared storage.

11. B. Templates are definitely what you would want to use to deploy the new virtual machines. Templates provide a way to share only the configuration of a virtual machine with new virtual machines. The other options take longer or are not a good fit.

12. A. Once a vCenter cluster is created with high availability, which requires vCenter Server, it is an easy task to configure virtual machine monitoring so that your virtual machines have built-in HA.

13. D. The definition fits only vCenter Operations Manager. This is the only VMware product that gives you a virtual representation of health.

14. D. Storage vMotion is the best way to move virtual machines on local storage to the shared storage on a SAN. Although you can copy the virtual machine files to shared storage, the process would be more involved. Storage vMotion was created to address challenges including moving to shared storage (among other things).

15. B. Although you can move selected virtual machines to the new storage, the easiest way to spread the virtual machines' files across new SAN volumes would be to leverage Storage DRS.

Storage I/O Control does not move virtual machine files; it is a way to control storage I/O. And vMotion does not move the virtual machines' files at all.

16. B. By far the biggest advantage is server consolidation. This is the driving force that allows higher physical server utilization while maintaining application isolation.

17. B. vCenter Site Recovery Manager makes short work of a disaster-recovery test. In fact, you can test site recovery easily. The hardware does not need to be the same as the original, and the storage does not have to be the same either.

18. A. Thin provisioning is a wonderful way to leverage SAN storage space. With thin provisioning, only the actual space with data is used. However, you do have to keep in mind when overcommitting any storage space to keep an eye on actual space used and running out of disk space completely.

19. A. Storage DRS will balance virtual machines across available SAN storage for you. Storage DRS leverages Storage vMotion to do its job. vMotion does not move files stored on SAN volumes (or local volumes). vCenter SRM is used for disaster recovery.

20. A. After converting a physical server into a virtual server, no changes are necessary. You should note, though, that you *can* change things. For example, if the local disks on the physical server have a lot of free space, you can resize the virtual disks during the conversion process so that they use less space.

Chapter 4

1. A. Physical storage is the underlying physical hardware that provides storage to the virtual environment.

2. D. Storage vMotion is used to move virtual machine files from one shared datastore to another without an outage on the virtual machine. VM storage profiles are used to move virtual machine files from one shared datastore to another based on the performance level of the datastore.

3. C. Local storage is storage that is contained within the ESXi host and is not easily shared across ESXi hosts. To share local disks to other ESXi hosts, you would need to use the vSphere Storage Appliance or a third-party option.

4. D. Disk zeroing is the process of changing each bit on a storage drive to a zero to make sure that no old data exists on the disk.

5. D. iSCSI and Network File System both use a standard network connection to connect an ESXi host to external storage. Fibre Channel uses a specialized network based on host bus adapter cards and fiber-optic switches.

6. A. Because thick provision eager zeroed drives are fully zeroed when they are created, they do not have to perform zeroing, which takes time, during production writes.

7. A. A raw device mapping allows a virtual machine to have direct access to an external storage device. It can be used to allow a virtual machine to have more control over a physical drive.

8. A. Storage vMotion can be used to migrate a running virtual machine's files from one datastore to another. This operation can be repeated for all the virtual machines on a datastore to clear it for maintenance.

9. B. Performance on a thin provisioned drive can be lower than on a thick provisioned drive, making critical high-performance environments not ideal for thin provisioned drives.

10. C. Disk provisioning can occur when creating a new virtual machine, adding a new drive to an existing virtual machine, cloning an existing virtual machine, or using Storage vMotion to move a virtual machine to a different datastore.

11. C. The Virtual Machine File System (VMFS) is a file system designed by VMware that allows multiple ESXi hosts to have read-write access to the file system at the same time. It is designed for high performance and to provide optimal performance for virtual machines.

12. B. Thick provision lazy zeroed is the default disk provisioning type for newly created drives in VMware.

13. A. Since a thick provision eager zeroed drive is fully zeroed when it is created, it can take longer to add to a virtual machine than the other disk types that are not zeroed when they are created.

14. B. Virtual storage is an abstracted view of the storage that is available to the virtual environment presented to the ESXi hosts. Because the storage has been virtualized (abstracted), the ESXi hosts are not aware of the underlying hardware and see it only as available storage.

15. D. vMotion is used by DRS to move virtual machines from one ESXi host to another when balancing virtual machine workloads. Storage vMotion and Storage DRS move virtual machine files from one datastore to another, and high availability (HA) does not use vMotion when it restarts virtual machines on other ESXi hosts.

16. D. Both thick provision eager zeroed and thick provision lazy zeroed use all the space on the datastore that they are allocated when they are created. Only thin provision disks start out small and consume space as it is needed.

17. B. Fibre Channel is a shared storage technology that connects the ESXi hosts to a storage array by using special cards called host bus adapters. Local storage uses the internal disk adapters to connect to the drives, and both iSCSI and Network File System use standard network cards.

18. B. Site Recovery Manager is a VMware disaster-recovery solution that can restore an entire data center with the pressing of a few buttons. It also allows live testing of the disaster-recovery plan.

19. C. vMotion is used to move running virtual machines from one ESXi host to another with no downtime for the virtual machine.

20. C. Shared storage is storage that is available to multiple ESXi hosts at the same time and is usually contained in storage arrays that are external to the ESXi hosts.

Chapter 5

1. D. Only a virtual switch would be used for routing VMkernel traffic with a port group. This is a VMware virtual construct.

2. B. The MAC address is used for layer 2 switching by a virtual switch. The same is true for a physical switch.

3. D. If a virtual switch gets a network packet from a virtual machine with a destination MAC address that it does not know, it hands off the packet to the uplink port connected to the port group for routing.

4. A. When you create a port group, you specify what you are going to use the switch for. You can choose between VMkernel traffic and virtual machine traffic.

5. D. A port group configured for VMkernel can do a lot, but it cannot be used for virtual machine network traffic.

6. C. A physical switch keeps track of the MAC address of traffic going though it in order to route packets effectively. Option D is close, but the packet is not sent out of the port that the packet came from.

7. B. The VMkernel connection type is used for storage, among other things. There are two types available: VMkernel and virtual machine traffic. You make this selection when you create the port group. You cannot choose both.

8. B. A physical switch does not dynamically expand the number of port connections as a virtual switch does. However, both types know about MAC addresses, route traffic between ports, and are required to talk on the network.

9. C. A standard virtual switch is all that is needed to route network traffic between these virtual servers. However, you need one installed locally on each of three hosts. So, three is the correct answer.

10. D. You need Enterprise Plus licensing to create the vNetwork Distributed Switch (vDS).

11. A. Distributed filters can filter bidirectionally. This is one of the neat features of the distributed virtual switch.

12. A. The Network Health Check keeps your environment free of configuration errors. Parameters for MTU, VLAN, and adapter teaming are checked.

13. D. When you connect two or more cards, as uplinks, to a virtual switch, you manage the aggregate, referred to as link aggregation. This is similar to managing CPUs and memory on ESXi hosts.

14. C. NetFlow and port mirroring are used by network administrators to troubleshoot virtual machines' network traffic. These are tools that can peer into the network activity of a virtual machine, much as a sniffer can peer into a physical server.

15. C. Distributed virtual switches should consist of at least one distributed virtual port group and one distributed virtual uplink.

16. B. The best analogy is a physical switch. An uplink connects the virtual switch to the physical network, not a port group.

17. A. Virtual switches route the same kind of packets as physical switches. This makes sense and is the easiest way to replace physical switches with virtual switches.

18. D. Virtual switches are layer 2 networking devices. Some physical switches do both layer 2 and layer 3 switching.

19. C. You don't have to do anything. The configuration of the number of ports on the port group will dynamically adjust to support the increased number of virtual machines.

20. B. vCenter Server is the only thing you must have to create a virtual switch. ESXi, as well as standard or physical switches, are not required.

Chapter 6

1. A. Fault tolerance creates a mirror of a running virtual machine, and as changes are made to the original virtual machine, they are also made to the mirror. If the original virtual machine fails, the mirror takes over with no downtime.

2. D. vMotion can be used to migrate all of the virtual machines off an ESXi host with no downtime so maintenance can be performed on the ESXi host.

3. D. A new virtual machine can be created for each application to provide application isolation. Multiple virtual machines could run on the same physical ESXi host so XYZ Corp. would not experience significantly increased hardware costs.

4. A. The vSphere storage appliance can be used to aggregate unused disks on ESXi hosts and use them as shared storage. This is effective for branch offices that do not have shared storage.

5. B. Distributed Power Management uses vMotion and wake-on-LAN technologies to save energy by powering off ESXi hosts when the demand for virtual machines is low and powering them back on as the demand increases. A good example of this would be a company that operates at its peak for the regular business day and has a reduced demand during the remainder of the day and in the evening. During the off-hours, the ESXi hosts would be kept in a low-power state, which would result in the company using less power and saving money.

6. B. Templates can be made from a model virtual machine and used to rapidly deploy a large number of similarly configured virtual machines. The templates can include the operating system as well as applications that need to be installed. Templates can greatly reduce the time it takes to deploy new virtual machines.

7. D. vMotion can be used to migrate a running virtual machine from one ESXi host to another without any disruption to the virtual machine and no downtime.

8. C. vCenter Configuration Manager is a VMware solution for monitoring virtual environments for configuration changes and alerting on them. It is extremely useful for companies in highly regulated industries.

9. B. High availability is a VMware technology that restarts virtual machines on a new host if the host they are currently running on fails. It does cause a small amount of downtime for the virtual servers, but it is only the length of time that it takes the virtual machines to restart on the new host and does not require any interaction from administrators.

10. A. Distributed Switch with QoS allows the network traffic of certain virtual machines to be prioritized over other virtual machines running on the same ESXi host to make sure they are running optimally.

11. B. Memory ballooning is a VMware technology that allows unused memory to be reclaimed from virtual machines when the memory demand of the virtual machines running on an ESXi host is high. Memory ballooning will only reclaim unused memory and does not adversely affect the virtual machines.

12. B. Distributed Resource Scheduler is a VMware technology that load balances virtual machines across ESXi hosts to remove the problem of hot spots, whereby one ESXi host is overused while others go underutilized.

13. C. Thin provisioning allows virtual machines to conserve disk space by consuming only the amount of space they need and expanding as more space is required. New drives can be configured for thin provisioning when they are created, and existing drives can be converted to thin provisioning by performing a Storage vMotion and specifying thin provisioning as the disk type.

14. D. vCenter Server is a VMware management tool that can be used to manage your entire virtual environment from one location. It is the primary tool you will use to make changes to your virtual environment and to manage it on a day-to-day basis.

15. C. Storage vMotion can be performed on each virtual machine located on the LUNs that are scheduled to be decommissioned, to move the virtual machines to new LUNs without any downtime. The LUNs could also be placed into maintenance mode, and vCenter will automatically use Storage vMotion to clear all the virtual machines from the LUNs.

16. D. vSphere Replication is a hardware-independent technology that allows running virtual machines to be replicated to another site to allow higher availability. If the original site is down due to a disaster, an up-to-date copy of the virtual machine could be brought online at the replication site.

17. C. Snapshots allow a point-in-time recovery point for a virtual machine. If a snapshot is taken before an upgrade or patching, and a failure occurs, the virtual machine can be quickly reverted back to the point of the snapshot.

18. C. Storage I/O Control (SIOC) allows the storage traffic of certain virtual machines to be prioritized, to make sure they are running optimally.

19. C. Site Recovery Manager is a VMware disaster-recovery solution that can restore an entire data center with the pressing of a few buttons. It can be easily configured and allows live testing of the disaster-recovery plan without affecting the production environment.

20. C. Transparent page sharing is a VMware technology that allows an ESXi host to better utilize its available memory by comparing the memory blocks of virtual machines and keeping any identical blocks in only one location. Virtual machines that are running the same operating system will have many memory blocks that are identical to memory blocks on other virtual machines. Transparent page sharing can keep only one copy of these identical memory blocks and therefore save memory that can be used for other virtual machines.

Online Resources

This book would not be complete without going over some of the online resources that would be very beneficial to anyone planning to take the VCAD510 test. We will go over the VMware resources first, since they are the most important. Then we'll look at some tips for using Google searches for efficient test prep.

VMware Resources

Since VMware created the VCAD510 test, it only makes sense that good information would come from the VMware site. Let's go over some of that now.

Documenation

When you are getting ready to take any VMware test, the first thing to look at is the exam blueprint. It will give you all of the objectives to learn and what you can expect on the test, how to register, what constitutes a passing score, and what the time limits are.

To go hand in hand with the e-learning course is the VMware vSphere Basics guide. The basics guide is only 38 pages long, and covers some of the same things in the e-learning course, but it's worth the read. The more exposure you get to the fundamentals of VMware virtualization, the better off you will be when taking the VCAD510 test. I suggest you print out the exam blueprint as well as the VMware vSphere Basics PDF file so that you can read the material any time. You can find the PDF here:

```
http://pubs.vmware.com/vsphere-50/topic/com.vmware.ICbase/PDF/vsphere-esxi-
vcenter-server-50-basics-guide.pdf
```

The VMware Virtualization Toolkit expands on your knowledge with videos, ROI calculators and a link to a 60-day evaluation, and PDF files:

- What's New in VMware vSphere 5.0: Storage
- What's New in VMware vSphere 5.0: Networking
- ESG Whitepaper: Raising Data Centers Closer to the Cloud
- Taneja Whitepaper: Optimizing Data Protection Operations
- Competitive Reviewers Guide
- Taneja Whitepaper: The True Cost of Virtual Server Solutions

The VMware Virtualization Toolkit is especially useful if you need documentation to help you get your company to buy into VMware virtualization. The storage and networking PDF files will be more beneficial to you for test preparation than the other documentation in the toolkit. To get the toolkit, just register at

`http://www.vmware.com/virtualization101_register`

> After registering, the toolkit is presented as a web page with links to information and tools. The Free 60-day Evaluation link details states that you can download your evaluation of VMware vSphere 4, including vSphere Enterprise Plus, vCenter Server Standard, and vCenter Server Heartbeat. But, don't worry; when you follow the links provided by the kit, you are directed to the new versions.

Downloading the product evaluation and going through an installation and configuration is one of the best ways to become really familiar with the product. The exam blueprint does mention that you should spend some hands-on time. And, for most people, adding hands on experience with anything will always provide knowledge that is more likely to stay with you.

The exam blueprint mentions "The Business Value of Virtualization" document, which is just the lowdown on how much virtualization helps businesses. This is definitely a document you would use to get buy-in from upper management on virtualization. The document goes into detail on what problems IT infrastructures have and how virtualization helps. It is more useful for getting the buy-in from management than it is for the VCAD510 test. But the concepts are useful. The "Business and Financial Benefits of Virtualization" document is much the same.

The "What's New in VMware vSphere" documents are must-reads. These can bring you up to speed quickly on some very advanced VMware technology. In particular, the vSphere 5.5

Networking document is a great eight-page short on the newest feature enhancements. The nice thing is, the document is short since it is only covering the newest features. However, the newest features seem to always find a spot in the test questions.

Here is the one web address that will always point to the new, correct documentation for all things VMware:

`https://www.vmware.com/support/pubs/`

Classes

It is recommended that you take the VMware Data Center Virtualization Fundamentals e-learning course before taking the test: `http://mylearn.vmware.com/register.cfm?course=189018`. The course gives you an overview of virtualization and does a really good job of getting you up to speed on the vocabulary. You do have to register with VMware to sign up for the course, but the course is free.

If you want to take a paid class for VMware, it is helpful if you know which track you want to go down. If you bought this book to take the VCAD510 test, you don't have to decide on any track for now. The VCAD510 test is just to get you acquainted with VMware virtualization in general. There are four tracks:

- Data center virtualization
- Cloud
- End-user computing
- Network virtualization

You should start thinking about which track interests you after you get the VCAD510 certification. There is no real need to take any paid class to take the VCAD510 test. This book gives you the basic knowledge you need. Coupled with the documentation and resources in this chapter, you can't lose.

Video

There is a lot of video on VMware products available. VMware Education Services has a centralized location for videos: http://www.vmwarecertificationvideos.com/. Click on All Videos to see the complete list. For the VCAD510 test, this site has a good overview of the certification, including benefits of the certification to you and your company, as well as letting you know what other resources are available to you from VMware that you can leverage for certification. Many other videos provide information on more in-depth certifications.

Using Google for Exam Preparation

Many people do not realize how a good Google search can make short work of many objectives. Like getting ready for this test. The following are a few things to help you to use Google effectively.

Quotation Marks   Putting quotes around your search term can be obvious and exactly what you need. A search for **VMware Certified Associate** without enclosing the term in quotation marks will give you half a million hits. But, with the quotes, it will give you only 68 thousand, and, what you get back is more useful for the test.

Filetype: Using the filetype operator will limit the results to specific file types. The most useful in our case is the PDF file type. Or, possibly PPT for PowerPoint presentations. One example to try is **VMware Certification Test filetype:pdf.**

Site: and -Site: What if you only want results from the VMware mothership? You can add a *site:vmware.com* to your search query and all the results will be from the VMware site. Conversely, if you wanted to exclude the VMware site, you would Google *-site:vmware.com* (simply including a minus symbol at the start) and nothing from vmware.com will show up in the search results. Don't forget the colon in these operators.

The following images show the difference between these two searches in the number of results.

Intitle: Intitle: is one of the most important operators if you do any serious Google searches. Think of intitle: as the topic. I can't tell you how often I have spent time searching where adding **intitle:** narrowed the search down quickly. Do a search for **"VMware Certified Associate"** and then add **intitle:test**. It is amazing.

If you routinely spend a lot of time searching, it really makes sense to use at least these four tips. There are many more tips just a search away. If you like a web form–based way to do an advanced search, just go to https://www.google.com/advanced_search.

So, why waste time with crafting Google searches in this book? Because the Internet changes every day and it will help you to know how these searches work. Here are some queries that you will want to check out:

- "VMware Certified Associate" site:vmware.com
- "VMware Certified Associate" intitle:test
- "VMware Certified Associate" intitle:questions
- "VMware Certified Associate" filetype:pdf

For many Internet users YouTube is a frequent destination. It doesn't matter if you want to know how to make cupcakes, want to be entertained, or see how jet engines work, YouTube has it all. For visual learners, YouTube does contain very useful information from a VMware Certified Associate - Data Center Virtualization point of view.

Enter **"VMware Certified Associate" site:youtube.com** and the search query will return just YouTube matches. Like anything on the Internet, you have to weed through the junk, but there are some good nuggets there. I have watched some of these videos and some are quite good. The better your search, the less weeding is necessary.

You get the idea. Make sure to put *VMware Certified Associate* in quotes for this to work. All of these operators really narrow the results to useful web resources. The best part is that knowing how to search gives you the most relevant results possible.

One other very useful tool is the Search Tools feature at the Google search home page. I use this every day. Let's say you want to see only recent information on your search. You can limit your search to the last hour, last 24 hours, or the last week, month, or year. If you are tired of getting search results from years ago, this is a good option. After you search for something, there is a Search Tools link with a time dropdown that will give you the options mentioned. This is also useful when searching for breaking news.

Here is an example. After clicking Search Tools, new options open below.

Of course, we have only scratched the surface here. The best ways to search on Google has filled many books already. If you frequently perform searches on Google, read one of the good books on the best way to leverage search.

Index

Note to the reader: Throughout this index **boldfaced** page numbers indicate primary discussions of a topic. *Italicized* page numbers indicate illustrations.

W

Y

Free Online Learning Environment

Register on Sybex.com to gain access to the free online interactive learning environment and test bank to help you prepare for the VCA-DCV exam.

The online test bank includes:

Assessment Test to help you focus your study to specific objectives

Chapter Tests to reinforce what you learned

Practice Exams to test your knowledge of the material

Electronic Flashcards to reinforce your learning and provide last-minute test prep before the exam

Searchable Glossary gives you instant access to the key terms you'll need to know for the exam

Go to `http://sybextestbanks.wiley.com` to register and gain access to this comprehensive study tool package.

Glossary

A

application HA   High availability for applications. Deployed as a virtual appliance, applications are monitored and restarted if necessary.

application isolation   The concept that one application will not interfere with another application on a different virtual machine.

availability challenge   Anything that can cause an important application to become unavailable to the users who rely on it or that cause an outage to go on longer than absolutely necessary.

B

ballooning   *See* memory ballooning.

bare-metal hypervisor   This type of hypervisor is installed directly on a physical server. The other is host based.

C

Cisco Nexus 1000V   A third-party networking device that works with VMware and provides some advanced functionality.

cluster   A logical grouping of ESXi hosts.

cold migration   The act of moving a virtual machine, which is powered off, to another ESXi host.

consolidation   Collapsing physical servers into fewer physical hosts running a hypervisor.

critical server   Any server in the environment that would cause a significant application outage if it failed.

D

data center   A root object defined in vCenter Server. Container for clusters.

datastore   A storage location for virtual machine files.

disaster recovery   The process of recovering systems and processes that have failed and are causing important applications or data to be unavailable.

disaster tolerance   *See* Disaster Recovery

disk provisioning   The process of creating a new disk or set of disks for a virtual machine.

disk zeroing   The process of changing each bit on a storage drive to a zero to make sure that no old data exists on the disk.

Distributed Power Management (DPM)   A VMware technology that allows companies to save electrical costs by powering off ESXi hosts when virtual machine demand is low and powering them back on as virtual machine demand increases.

Distributed Resource Scheduler (DRS)   A vSphere technology that evenly spreads virtual machine load across multiple ESXi hosts in a cluster. DRS also automatically decides which host to power a virtual machine on.

Distributed Switch with QoS   A VMware technology that allows the network traffic of certain virtual machines to be prioritized.

distributed virtual port groups   One of two technologies that make up a distributed switch. Distributed virtual port groups provide connections to the distributed virtual switch.

distributed virtual switch (dvSwitch)   A type of virtual switch that can be deployed once and attached to newly created ESXi hosts.

distributed virtual uplinks   Part of a distributed virtual switch and aggregating physical network connections of ESXi hosts. The other piece of a distributed switch. These are similar to standard virtual uplinks.

downtime   The amount of time that an application is unavailable due to a server or group of servers being offline. This includes both scheduled and unscheduled outages.

DPM   Acronym for *Distributed Power Management.*

DRS   Acronym for *Distributed Resource Scheduler.*

dvSwitch   Acronym for *distributed virtual switch.*

F

fault tolerance (FT)   A VMware technology that allows a mirror to be created of a running virtual machine. As changes are made to the original virtual machine, they are also made to the mirror. If the original virtual machine fails, the mirror takes over without any application downtime.

forged transmits   This technology compares effective Mac addresses and source Mac addresses of network traffic from virtual machines. Basically, a virtual machine impersonating a different MAC address.

FT   Acronym for *fault tolerance.*

H

HA   Acronym for *high availability*.

high availability (HA)   A VMware technology that is used to restart virtual machines on a different ESXi host if the ESXi host they are on fails.

hosted hypervisor   A hypervisor that is installed on an operating system as an application. VMware Workstation is a good example of a hosted hypervisor.

hot add   A VMware technology that allows CPUs and memory to be added to running virtual machines without downtime.

hot spot   A datastore or ESXi host on the network that is overburdened while other datastores or ESXi hosts are being underutilized.

hypervisor   A type of traffic cop that provides virtualized hardware for virtual machines and talks to the physical hardware. ESXi is a hypervisor.

L

link aggregation   Pooling network links on a host or group of hosts. Two 1 GB network uplinks could be aggregated into one 2 GB network link, for instance.

M

MAC address   A unique identifier for the physical network card. Used to keep track of network communications on a layer 2 networking level.

management challenge   An issue that causes the virtual environment to become harder to manage or fully understand.

memory ballooning   A VMware technology that allows unused memory that is being held by a virtual machine to be reclaimed and used by other virtual machines.

N

NetFlow   A protocol on Cisco routers used to collect IP network traffic as it goes in and out of a network interface.

network vMotion   A network vMotion is the same as a regular vMotion but with the added benefit of keeping network statistics.

NSX   VMware advanced network and security virtualization platform.

O

optimization challenge   Anything that can cause applications to run at less-than-peak performance or can cause resources to be wasted.

P

P2V   A migration, usually using VMware converter, from a physical server or workstation to a virtual machine.

physical storage   The underlying physical hardware that provides storage to the virtual environment.

port group   A major part of a virtual switch used to group virtual machines' network configurations.

port mirroring   The practice of mirroring network traffic going to a port in an effort to monitor network communications. Also known as a *switched port analyzer.*

private VLAN   Also known as *private ports*, a private VLAN isolates ports as a way to further segment VLAN traffic.

promiscuous mode   The configuration of a virtual machine's network port to listen in on all packets going over the network, even ones that aren't sent directly to it.

Q

QoS   Acronym for *quality of service.*

quality of service (QoS)   Quality of Service is a technology that guarantees certain levels of service for throughput, transit delay, and packet priority on a network.

R

raw device mapping (RDM)   A virtual drive pointer in VMware that points to a raw physical storage device.

RDM   Acronym for raw device mapping.

resource pools   Used to partition available CPU and memory resources.

right-sizing   The process of identifying virtual machines that have more CPU or memory resources than they need and reducing these resources to decrease waste.

S

SAN   Acronym for storage area network.

scalability challenge   Anything that can cause issues as a company's infrastructure continues to grow or limits the company's ability to quickly meet new challenges.

sDRS   Acronym for *Storage DRS.*

shared storage   Storage that can be accessed by multiple ESXi hosts.

SIOC   Acronym for *Storage I/O Control.*

Site Recovery Manager (SRM)   A VMware disaster-recovery solution that can restore an entire data center with the pressing of a few buttons.

snapshots   *See* virtual machine snapshots.

SRM   Acronym for *Site Recovery Manager.*

storage area network (SAN)   A specialized network for sharing storage resources such as disk arrays.

Storage DRS (sDRS)   A VMware technology that allows virtual machine files to be load balanced across storage arrays to avoid Hot Spots.

Storage I/O Control (SIOC)   A VMware technology that allows the storage traffic of certain virtual machines to be prioritized to make sure they are running optimally.

Storage vMotion (svMotion)   A VMware technology that can be used to migrate all the virtual machines off a storage array with no downtime so maintenance can be performed on the storage array.

svMotion   Acronym for *Storage vMotion.*

T

template   *See* virtual machine template.

thick provision eager zeroed   A type of disk provisioning in which the entire drive is allocated and zeroed when it is initially created.

thick provision lazy zeroed   A type of disk provisioning in which the entire drive is allocated when it is initially created but is not zeroed until it is used.

Thin provisioning   A VMware technology that allows virtual machines to conserve disk space by consuming only the amount of space they actually need and expanding as more space is needed.

traffic filtering Stopping certain network traffic based on the traffic attributes.

traffic shaping A way to intelligently route network traffic based on quality of service or other factors.

transparent page sharing A VMware technology that allows an ESXi host to better utilize its available memory by comparing the memory blocks of virtual machines and keeping any identical blocks in only one location.

U

upgrade To add additional resources to a virtual machine or to install a newer version of software.

uplink port group A group of physical network connections grouped together and used as resources for virtual machines.

V

V2V A migration of a virtual machine to a virtual machine. The destination virtual machine could be on a different platform.

vApp Virtual application; a container object in the vCenter Server hierarchy that contains virtual machines acting as one.

VCCM Acronym for *vCenter Configuration Manager.*

vCenter Configuration Manager (VCCM) A VMware solution for monitoring virtual environments for configuration changes.

vCenter Operations Manager (vCOPS) A VMware product that can be used to identify performance bottlenecks in the virtual environment and to provide metrics on the virtual machines that can be used to perform virtual machine right-sizing.

vCenter Server A VMware product that acts as a centralized management tool for VMware virtualization infrastructures.

vCOPS Acronym for *vCenter Operations Manager.*

VDP Acronym for *vSphere Data Protection.*

vFlash A VMware technology that allows virtual machines to use solid-state drives on the ESXi host as their cache to increase performance and reduce the impact of memory swapping.

virtual machine A software representation of a physical server that can perform all of the same functions as a physical server and has advantages that physical servers lack. *Virtual machine* is synonymous with *virtual server.*

virtual machine snapshots   A VMware technology that allows a point-in-time recovery point for a virtual machine to be created.

virtual machine template   A VMware technology for rapidly deploying virtual servers by taking an image of a model virtual server and using it to deploy a large number of similar virtual machines.

virtual server   A software representation of a physical server that can perform all of the same functions as a physical server and has advantages that physical servers lack. *Virtual server* is synonymous with *virtual machine*.

virtual storage   An abstract view of the storage that is available to the virtual environment presented to the ESXi hosts.

virtual switch   A virtual version of a physical switch. A virtual switch can route communications for a virtual environment.

VM storage profiles   A VMware technology that provides an automated way to ensure that virtual machines are running on storage that has the performance level they require to perform optimally.

vMotion   A VMware technology that can be used to migrate all the virtual machines off an ESXi host with no downtime so maintenance can be performed on the ESXi host.

vNetwork Distributed Switch (vDS)   A vNetwork Distributed Switch (available in Enterprise Plus and above licenses) is used to consistently configure VMware resources, such as standard virtual switches, on a data center–wide level.

VSA   Acronym for *VMware Storage Appliance*.

vSphere Data Protection   A VMware solution for backing up and restoring virtual machines.

vSphere Orchestrator   A VMware product used to automate manual processes. vSphere Orchestrator can interact with vCenter, AD, PowerShell, and other technologies to automate repeatable tasks.

vSphere Replication   A hardware-independent VMware technology that allows running virtual machines to be replicated to another site to allow higher availability.

vSphere Storage Appliance (VSA)   A VMware technology that can be used to aggregate unused disks on ESXi hosts and use them as shared storage.

W

wake-on-LAN   A technology that allows physical servers to be powered on remotely.